Turkish Wine
A Heritage Reborn

From Olus to Vinolus

# Turkish Wine
## A Heritage Reborn

### From Olus to Vinolus

© All rights reserved. No part of this publication may be reproduced, stored in a retrieval system, or transmitted in any form or by any means, electronic, mechanical, photocopying, recording, or otherwise, without the prior written permission of the copyright owner.

**1st edition:** 1000 English copies; October 2024

**ISBN** 978-3-99029-665-3

**Editors**
Inanc Atilgan & Bronwen Batey
inanc.atilgan@gmail.com

**Publishing**
Wieser Verlag AUSTRIA

**Book Design**
Erdoğan Yavuz & Mustafa Yavuz

**Printing & Binding**
Grafiker - Ankara / TÜRKİYE

**Photographs & Illustrations**
Ağaoğlu [78]
Atış [64]
Atılgan [8, 9, 12, 14, 18, 26, 34, 38, 40, 48, 50, 51, 52, 57, 58, 62, 66, 68, 82, 84, 88, 92]
Batey [11]
Gündoğan [22, 24, 28, 29]
Istanbul University Library [60]
JRE [94]
Kutluay [6, 16, 17, 32, 54 (left)]
Molu [30, 32 (right), 33, 36, 42, 43, 45, 46, 47, 55, 61, 72, 80, 81, 86, 87, 91, 96]
Serim [73]
Winkler [20]

# Turkish Wine
## A Heritage Reborn

## From Olus to Vinolus

Dr. Inanc Atilgan & Bronwen Batey DipWSET

Wieser Verlag

Grafiker

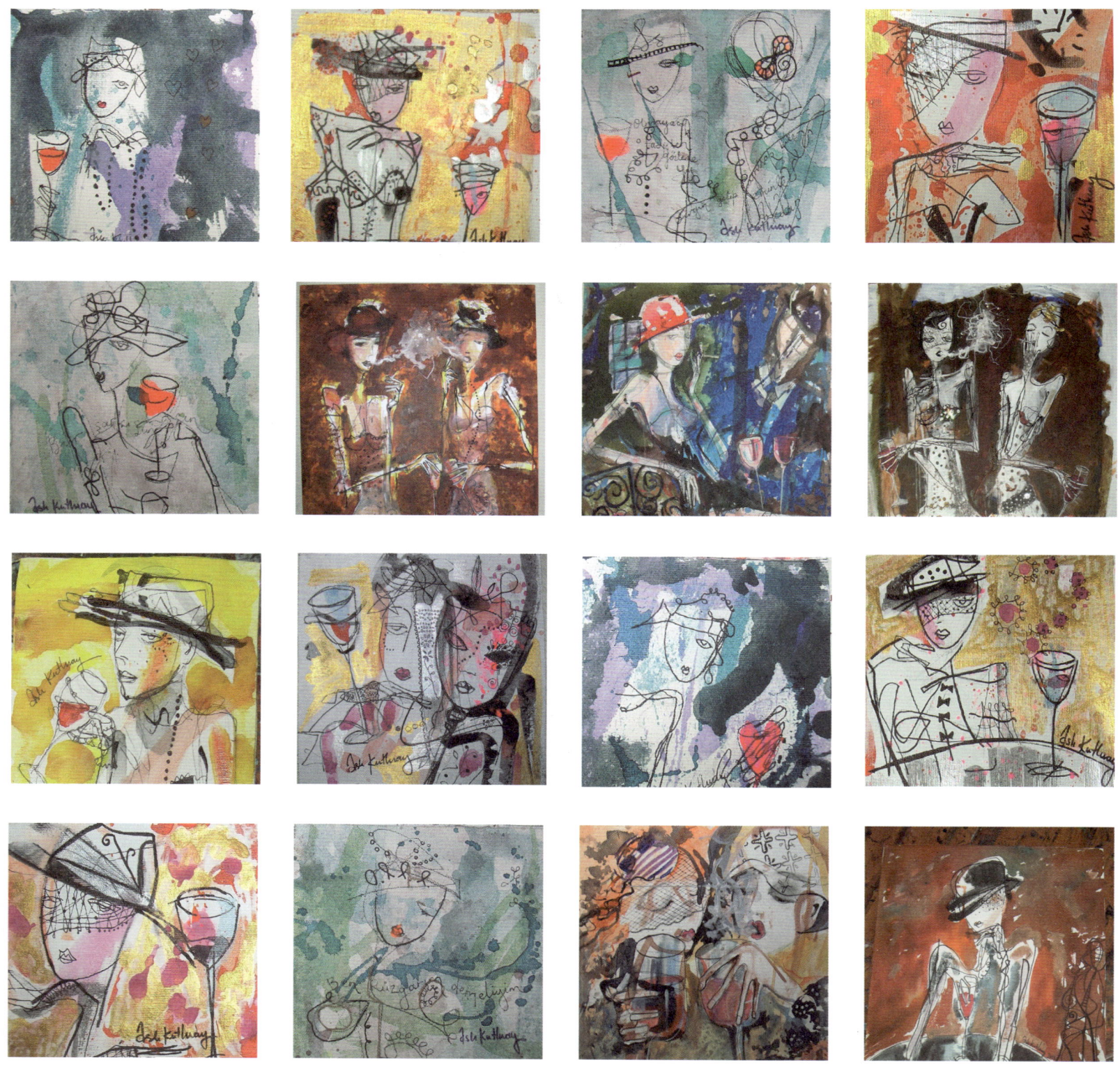

Aslı Kutluay: **How to Illustrate Wine** (Painter)

# Contents

İnanç Atılgan & Bronwen Batey, *Editors*
Introduction ... 9

Susanne Kraus-Winkler, *Austrian State Secretary for Tourism*
Understanding Vinolus and Cappadocian Wines ... 13

Lojze Wieser, *Professor, three times winner of "The Best City Cookbook in the World"*
A Journey to Rediscovered Flavours. The Boutique Wines of Anatolia ... 19

Göknur Gündoğan, *PhD, Author, Wine Expert*
Turkish Wine Reloaded ... 23

Mehmet Şahin, *President of Erciyes University a.d.*
The Molu Family and Oluş ... 31

José Hernández, *Vinolus Oenologist and Co-owner of Heraki Wines in Türkiye*
VINOLUS by José ... 35

Jorg Zupan, *Michelin Star & JRE Member Chef*
My Experience with Vinolus in Cappadocia: A Culinary Journey of Flavours ... 39

Azra Seyok, *Chairwoman of the Board of Directors, Karsu Textile*
The Productive and Sustainable World of my Sister, Oluş ... 43

Perisa Kastratovic, *State Secretary at the Ministry of Foreign Affairs of Montenegro and former Ambassador to Türkiye*
Gastrodiplomacy and Oluş ... 49

Aysu İnsel, *Professor of Economics*
Oluş Molu: Exploring the Journey of an Extraordinary Leader in Sustainable Farming and Holistic Living ... 55

İnanç Atılgan, *Cultural Scientist, JRE Representative to Türkiye*
Perception of Champagne Among The Ottoman Elite ... 59

Süray Cingöz Atış & Doğuhan Atış, *Wine Experts, Owners of Santé Wine & More*
From Vine to Wine: The Journey of Vinolus in Anatolia ... 65

Pınar Akkaya *DipWSET*
Multicultural Background of Oluş and Its Impact on Vinolus ... 69

Sabit Ağaoğlu, *Professor of Agriculture and Owner of Tomurcukbağ Wines*
The Rediscovery and Revival of Kalecik Karası: When Knowledge is Nurtured by Love ... 79

Gözdem Gürbüzatik, *Fermented and Distilled Beverages Strategist. Heritage Vines of Turkey Co-founder*
Seeing the Unseen in Türkiye: A Precarious Heritage for Humanity ... 83

Yasemin Altınyay, *International Banker*
Economic Potential of the Turkish Wine Industry: From a Historical Perspective to a Future Scenario ... 89

Hans van Manen, *Secretary General of the JRE*
The Essence of Wine in Fine Dining ... 93

Terracotta beaker in the shape of a bunch of grapes from Kültepe in Kayseri (19th-17th century B.C.), exhibited in the Museum of Anatolian Civilisations in Ankara.

# Introduction

Over a thousand years ago, Turks migrated from Central Asia to what is now Anatolia and Southeastern Europe. In their new homeland, they merged their own culture into the existing civilisations, creating a dynamic, discerning, and harmonious identity where being influenced, as well as being the influencer is viewed as a cultural richness. A Turk is multifaceted; an Asian, a European, connected to an international society. This polygonal identity is reflected in their palate, cuisine, and beverages.

These unique traits of Turkish culture have provided an exciting backdrop for the production of surprising and impressive wines. In Türkiye's pre-Islamic and Islamic periods, wine held significant importance. The old Turkish word for wine is generally accepted as "süçig", which means "sweet, wine"; a word used in pre-Islamic and early Islamic times. Alcohol, as in many other cultures across the world plays an important role in Turkish culture. Turks have retained and enriched the wine culture passed down from the non-Muslim communities they lived alongside, such as Armenians, Greeks, Levantines, and Assyrians, and they endeavour to preserve it despite the pervasive political and social turmoil.

Türkiye is home to a rich array of indigenous grape varieties. Grapes such as Öküzgözü, Boğazkere, Kalecik Karası, and Narince distinguish Turkish wines from those of other countries, contributing to a sense of terroir and a distinct uniqueness in flavour profiles. This rich diversity, coupled with Türkiye's varied topography and climate, offers a wide range of terroirs for grape cultivation, from the Aegean and Mediterranean coasts to the central Anatolian plateau.

In recent years, there has been a renewed focus on modernising winemaking techniques and improving overall quality, resulting in a growth of Turkish wineries producing internationally competitive wines. Gaining recognition and awards in global wine competitions, these wines have supported an increasingly positive perception of Turkish wine. The rise of wine tourism has also played a role in shaping Türkiye's image as a renowned wine region, welcoming visitors to vineyards, wineries and wine festivals.

Based in Vienna, İnanç lectures on gastronomy, exploring its historical and etymological aspects, at universities in both Türkiye and Austria

Turkish winemaking is indeed experiencing a revival, buoyed by the growth in grape varieties, the number of producers, consumption, and especially the increase in quality recognised at an international level. At the forefront of this renaissance is Vinolus, a shining example of the progress and potential of Turkish wine culture. This book is dedicated to celebrating the achievements of Vinolus, an extraordinary success story brought to life by Oluş Molu in the heart of Anatolia, Cappadocia. Through Vinolus, our aim is to showcase Türkiye as an exciting, thriving wine region supported by its evolving wine culture.

Experts in their fields and thought leaders in gastronomic culture have contributed to this book. What binds them is their close acquaintance with Oluş and Türkiye.

Professor Wieser, three times winner of "The Best City Cookbook in the World" compares Türkiye's ancient winemaking traditions, tracing back thousands of years with the recent revival of these practices by local winemakers like those at Vinolus, with a particular emphasis on how they are appealing to the European palate.

Süray Cingöz Atış and Doğuhan Atış renowned for their success story of Santé Wine & More in Istanbul, discuss the transformation of Vinolus, focusing on Oluş's dedication to organic farming and production of high-quality wines.

Oluş's sister, Azra Seyok reflects on their family's legacy in agriculture and how it has influenced Oluş's approach to organic farming and sustainable viticulture. She highlights how Oluş blends her family heritage with modern environmental practices to produce exceptional Turkish wines.

Professor İnsel provides insight into Oluş's character and her commitment to sustainable living, praising Oluş's leadership in promoting organic farming and her innovative contributions to Turkish wine culture.

Gözdem Gürbüzatik, one of the leading managers of alcoholic beverages in Türkiye, discusses the rich heritage of Turkish viticulture, focusing on efforts to preserve and promote Türkiye's indigenous grape varieties through unique innovations and initiatives.

Dr. Atılgan explores the historical context of wine and champagne consumption among the Ottoman elite, highlighting the cultural and religious complexities surrounding alcohol in Ottoman society.

Göknur Gündoğan, one of the leading wine specialists in Türkiye, provides an overview of the geographical and historical significance of viticulture in Türkiye, emphasising the country's potential in the global wine industry.

José Hernández, the Oenologist of Vinolus, discusses his journey to Türkiye to work with Oluş to produce wines that reflect the unique characteristics of Cappadocia's vineyards. He highlights the challenges of making wine in the region, and Oluş's pioneering work in organic wine production.

Perisa Kastratovic, State Secretary at the Ministry of Foreign Affairs of Montenegro and former Ambassador to Türkiye illustrates how Turkish wine can play an integral role in gastrodiplomacy. He affirms the role of Vinolus wines in showcasing Türkiye's rich and diverse culture, creating a positive impression on international guests.

Jorg Zupan, a Michelin-starred chef, shares his experience of pairing Turkish wines with Slovenian cuisine. He underscores the deep historical connections between Turkish and Balkan culinary traditions and praises the unique flavours of Vinolus wines, which reflect the rich terroir of Cappadocia.

Professor Şahin, biographer of the Molu family and former President of the Kayseri Erciyes University, provides a historical overview of the Molu family, emphasizing their deep roots in Kayseri and their transition from landowners to industrialists and eventually back to agriculture under the leadership of Oluş. The story of the Molu family reflects Türkiye's broader transformation, with Oluş reviving the family farm through organic agriculture and contributing significantly to Turkish viticulture.

Professor Ağaoğlu, the scientist who revived the Kalecik Karası grape and the owner of Tomurcukbağ Vineyard in Kalecik, details the rediscovery and revival of the Kalecik Karası grape variety, emphasising its historical importance and the scientific efforts that saved this indigenous grape from extinction. He praises Vinolus in particular for helping to elevate the status of Kalecik Karası both nationally and internationally.

Based in London, Bronwen is a freelance wine, food and travel writer, and a wine tourism marketing consultant with a passion for discovering new wines and wine regions.

Austrian State Secretary for Tourism, Susanne Kraus-Winkler, discusses her visit to Cappadocia and Vinolus, highlighting the region's rich winemaking tradition dating back to the Hittites . She notes the unique terroir of Cappadocia and the sustainable practices of Vinolus, which reflect a deep respect for the region's heritage.

As an international banker, Yasemin Altinyay examines the economic potential of the Turkish wine industry from a historical perspective, arguing that Türkiye's vast vineyard resources are currently underutilised for winemaking. She advocates for increasing the percentage of grape production dedicated to wine, which could significantly boost the country's economy.

Pinar Akkaya, holder of the world-renowned Wine & Spirits Education Trust Diploma, explores the multicultural background of Oluş and how it influences her winemaking at Vinolus. She describes how Oluş's diverse Turkish and German heritage influences and fuels her creativity and drives her to produce wines that reflect the rich cultural tapestry of Cappadocia. Pinar emphasises that Vinolus wines are not just beverages but are cultural artefacts that bridge different traditions and histories.

Hans van Manen, Secretary General of the JRE, describes how wine plays an integral role in the fine dining experience by complementing and enhancing the cuisine symbiotically. This is achieved through the close collaboration between chefs and sommeliers, ensuring that wine not only accompanies but elevates the gastronomic experience.

The overall message of these contributors centres on the profound cultural, historical, and economic significance of Turkish wine, currently being revived and transformed by visionary figures like Oluş Molu.

Overall, the stories are one of optimism and pride in Türkiye's wine heritage, combined with a forward-looking vision that embraces innovation, sustainability, and global engagement. The contributions collectively explore how Turkish wine is not just a beverage but a cultural treasure that embodies the rich history and diverse influences of Türkiye, and showcases its potential to play a significant role in the global wine industry.

Dr. İnanç Atılgan & Bronwen Batey DipWSET
30 August 2024, Vienna & London

# Understanding Vinolus and Cappadocian Wines: A Journey Through Türkiye's Ancient Vineyards

**Susanne Kraus-Winkler,** *Austrian State Secretary for Tourism*

*usanne and Oluş 'anding in front of the 'ehmet Şakir Paşa edrese in 'ustafapaşa/Cappadocia, onstructed in 1899. oday, this building serves a facility for the niversity of Cappadocia.*

Cappadocia enchants its visitors with its nature, history, caravanserais (roadside inns), churches, and villages. It is a fairy tale land of towers and caves formed by ancient volcanic eruptions and erosion.

Cappadocia bears traces of many cultures, from the Hittites to the Romans, Byzantines, Sassanids, Armenians, Seljuk Turks, Ottoman Turks, and finally the Turks of modern times. It is a crossroad, intersecting the Silk Road with the King's Road. Cappadocia in the heart of Türkiye is renowned for its otherworldly landscapes of magical chimneys and underground cities. It also holds a lesser-known but equally captivating secret: its ancient winemaking tradition. Nestled among its geological marvels are vineyards that have produced wine for millennia, making Cappadocian wines a fascinating subject for both connoisseurs and casual enthusiasts alike.

I had the opportunity to experience this as a guest at Oluş's vineyard, Vinolus. This was not only a unique chance to personally witness her significant contribution to Türkiye's wine culture but also to experience Cappadocia's great winemaking tradition, which dates back to the Hittite civilization of around 1800 BC. The Hittite language was deciphered as an Indo-European language by the Austrian-Czech linguist Bedřich Hrozný in 1915. Archaeological evidence suggests that viticulture was an integral part of daily life and religious rituals for the Hittites. The region's distinctive tufa soil, a soft volcanic rock, along with its unique microclimate is ideal for viticulture. This historical legacy has imbued Cappadocian wines with a rich heritage, linking modern winemakers to their ancient predecessors.

> **I had arrived at the cradle and birthplace of wine itself. Here I discovered a pioneer who enriches this culture with a woman's touch.**

The purpose of my visit to Vinolus was to discuss a tourism concept and collaboration between Austrian wine, organic farming, and architecture. Having over 40 years of experience in the hospitality industry, including hotel and restaurant management, tourism consulting, and academic lecturing, and as a founding partner of the LOISIUM Wine & Spa Resort Hotel Group, I was involved in creating the LOISIUM Wine World in one of Austria's top wine regions. This included establishing two wine and design hotels in Austria and two wine hotel projects in Champagne and Alsace. I visited Oluş to explore the possibility of launching a new project inspired by LOISIUM, called "LOISIUM Cappadocia."

We Austrians are passionate about wine and strive to nurture viticulture and winemaking. This is demonstrated by the importance we place on our own grape cultivation, our respect for nature through environmentally-friendly technology, and the unique wine tourism initiatives we foster. I approached Oluş to share these ideas, and I found that I had arrived at the cradle and birthplace of wine itself. Here, I discovered a pioneer who enriches this culture with a woman's touch. Oluş is a unique human being and a remarkable winemaker. She belongs to one of the oldest and most renowned families in Kayseri; according to her, the origins of thre Molu family can be traced back to the Dulkadirids, who existed from 1337 to 1522 AD. The Molu family also have direct commercial links to Austria. The KARSU Textile Factory, established by Oluş's family in 1973, is a direct partner with the Austrian company Lenzing AG, the world's largest producer of viscose fibres. In addition, many members of the Molu family speak German.

While savouring delicious Central Anatolian cuisine and sipping Vinolus wines at Oluş's home, she informed me how a combination of the soil, climate, and topography of Cappadocia's terroir plays a crucial role in creating the distinctive qualities found in her wines. The tufa soil is porous, providing excellent drainage while retaining much-needed moisture, vital for the vines during the dry summer months. The region's altitude, ranging from 800 to 1300 metres above sea level, contributes to significant diurnal temperature variations, enhancing the aromatic complexity and acidity of the grapes.

The white grape Emir from Cappadocia is perhaps the most renowned, and a key variety for Vinolus wines. Another is the black grape Kalecik Karası, known abroad as KK. Oluş's KK has won several national and international medals.

Vinolus is a small-scale winery focusing on sustainable viticulture and minimal intervention across the production process. Through this, Oluş aims to express the purest form of her vineyards' terroir and varietal expression of the grapes grown, creating wines that are distinctive and true to the region's heritage. Oluş positions herself at the heart of similar small, artisanal wineries in Türkiye. These boutique operations are usually family-owned and run, and prioritise quality over quantity. Boutique winemaking is characterised by meticulous attention to detail, from hand-harvesting grapes to small batch production processes, resulting in unique, high-quality wines that reflect the terroir and the winemaker's creativity. Oluş and her Vinolus are prime examples of this.

Cappadocia's unique appeal extends beyond its wines to offer a holistic experience for visitors. Wine tourism has become an integral part of the region's allure, with numerous vineyards opening their doors to tourists. One of them is Sunolus, Oluş's guesthouse at the vineyard. Visitors can explore the cellars of Vinolus, take part in guided tastings, and even participate in the grape harvest in autumn. This immersive experience provides a deeper understanding of the

*ustrian architect Brigitte eber, Berglandmilch ard Chairman Stefan ndner and Project eveloper Özkan emir discussing the tential location for e construction of the isium Cappadocia ject with Oluş.*

intricate relationship between Cappadocia's natural landscape and its viticultural practices, and a glimpse into Oluş's own special Cappadocia.

A unique synergy is created when you combine organic farming and boutique winemaking with a female producer. Cappadocia has recently experienced a renaissance in its agricultural and viticultural practices, driven by a growing emphasis on sustainability, tradition, and innovation. Championing this approach, Oluş is a perfect example and role model. This transformation is particularly evident in the realm of organic farming and boutique winemaking in Türkiye, with Oluş playing a pivotal role. The convergence of all of these elements—female leadership in agriculture, organic farming methods, and the rise of boutique wineries—creates a dynamic and collaborative force that is reshaping Türkiye's wine industry.

The future of Turkish winemaking is exciting, driven by the passion and dedication of innovative winemakers like Oluş who are committed to organic farming and low-intervention, small batch production. Their holistic approach ensures that the wines produced are not only of exceptional quality but also sustainable and reflective of Türkiye's rich agricultural heritage. As more consumers around the world seek out organic, artisanal wines made from unusual, indigenous grapes, the synergy between these elements positions Türkiye as a rising star in the global wine industry.

When an inspirational woman creates wine, the result is a blend of meticulous craftsmanship, a unique personal touch, and a deep respect for tradition and nature. Thank you, Oluş.

# A Journey to Rediscovered Flavours. The Boutique Wines of Anatolia

Prof. Lojze Wieser, *Publisher and three times winner of "The Best City Cookbook in the World"*

...sting of Vinolus, Kastro
...eli and Heraki wines by
...e founding members of
...e Netherlands-based
...ine Bridge Türkiye
...sociation" (WBT) in
...tzbühel in the Austrian
...os (Hotel Penzinghof).

My appreciation for the cuisine of the Balkans has led me to Türkiye, a country rich in history, culture, and viticulture on several occasions. During my visits, I have been fortunate to explore the history of the country's grapes and wines, in what is one of the largest grape-growing regions in the world, yet remarkably, barely recognised on the global wine map. In recent times, however, things have changed and local winemakers are starting to make a name for themselves, especially with artisanal wines. Today, Türkiye is an emerging player on the international wine scene, matching its unique and exciting wines and flavour profiles to a discerning European palate; and one that is constantly seeking diversity.

Inspired by Oluş Molu, the visionary behind the renowned Turkish wine brand Vinolus, I would like to offer my thoughts on how wines from this region are starting to enrich the European wine landscape once again.

Türkiye's winemaking tradition is ancient, with roots stretching back thousands of years to Anatolia, where the Hittites cultivated grapes as early as 1700 BC. One constant in the region's winemaking culture has been its historical challenges and associations with population shifts. Yet the people of the region have preserved, adopted and mastered these challenges into their assimilated communities.

> **Boutique wineries in Türkiye such as Vinolus are at the forefront of this revolution.**

Their long heritage of upheaval and knowledge building over millennia has evolved into today's modern winemaking culture in Türkiye.

Following the wave of privatisation in 2004, viticulture across Türkiye has been revitalised. Nearly 200 wineries are now rediscovering their native grape varieties and unique terriors. This renaissance is more than just a revival; it is an innovative integration of Türkiye's rich viticultural heritage into the global wine narrative.

Boutique wineries in Türkiye, such as Vinolus, are at the forefront of this revolution. With Oluş at the helm, the team at Vinolus are not just winemakers; they are artisans dedicated to crafting wines that reflect the unique terroir and cultural heritage of their land. Unlike large-scale commercial operations, many of Türkiye's smaller producers focus on quality rather than quantity, increasingly employing organic and sustainable farming methods, respecting the preservation of their local micro-terroir and environmental conditions.

Vinolus is considered to be a leader in modern winemaking in the beautiful region of Cappadocia. Oluş's wines are a showcase of quality, tradition, and innovation. Only with careful cultivation and pressing of the grapes can the distinctive and unique aromas and flavours be lifted from the grapes, highlighting what makes Turkish grapes genuinely unique in the world of wine. This has all been made possible via local, indigenous grape varieties such as Kalecik Karası, Boğazkere, Emir, and

Narince, only fairly recently rediscovered and recognised.

Sustainability has meanwhile become a byword at Turkish boutique wineries, especially those that have joined the association "Wine Bridge Türkiye" (WBT), founded in the Netherlands. WBT promotes organic production and places great value on sustainable practices in terroir-driven viticulture. Members of WBT, such as Vinolus, Kastro Tireli, and Heraki, adhere to these principles, prioritising not only safeguarding of the environment but also being mindful to use natural resources responsibly. By combining traditional methods with modern technology, the resulting wines are both authentic and innovative, whilst expressing the character of the region.

Despite Türkiye's rich winemaking history, winemakers today face significant challenges. The predominantly Muslim population of the country, along with Islamic prohibitions on alcohol consumption, present cultural hurdles. Furthermore, the emigration of non-Muslim communities that historically contributed to winemaking, and the lack of state support have negatively impacted or hindered the development of Turkish wines and the recognition of Türkiye as a genuine wine region. Nevertheless, through their innovative work, the country's boutique winemakers have transformed these obstacles into high-quality products.

The efforts of Turkish boutique wineries have contributed to a cultural renaissance in winemaking. Regularly recognised and awarded for their unique qualities, the appreciation and acknowledgement of Tükiye's artisanal wines can be seen at international competitions such as Decanter World Wine Awards (DWWA), International Wine Challenge (IWC), Concours Mondial de Bruxelles, Mundus Vini, and the International Wine & Spirit Competition (IWSC). Turkish wines have become a unique, interesting offering for connoisseurs of gastronomy and today, Türkiye is increasingly perceived not only as a leading producer of raisins and sultanas but more and more as a wine-producing country.

Little by little, the distinctive wines of Anatolia are inspiring the discerning European palate. By incorporating these wines into the international gastronomy scene, awareness for Turkish wines is becoming more refined, expanding the sensory repertoire of wine connoisseurs with their distinct notes and flavours, only enhanced by the history of Türkiye, including all of its highs and lows. The return of these unique wines, and their distinct flavour profiles is more than just a narrative; it shows, in its unique way, that what has disappeared often lives on, like an underground river, cleansing and renewing itself, and the loss of knowledge sprouts new buds with the capacity to enrich the entire European landscape. These wines and varieties may have been suppressed, but they were never forgotten. They have long been imprinted in one's Türkiye's own identity. It is these tangible and intangible sensory characteristics that make the world of wine so flavourful. Why forego any one of them!

> **The return of these unique wines and their distinct flavour profiles shows that what has disappeared often lives on like an underground river.**

# WINES OF TÜRKIYE

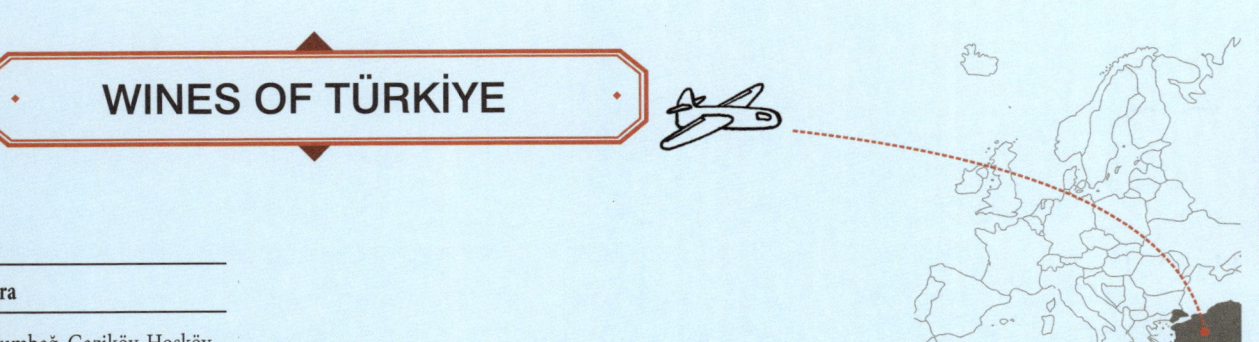

**White Grapes**
Chardonnay, Pinot Gris, Sauvignon Blanc, Muscat, Semillon, Riesling

**Black Grapes**
Cabernet Sauvignon, Merlot, Pinot Noir, Cabernet Franc, Syrah, Petit Verdot, Nero d'Avola, Sangiovese, Cinsault, Carignan, Alicante Bouschet, Gamay, Grenache

**Some Indigenous Grapes**
*(Black)* - Öküzgözü, Boğazkere, Kalecik Karası, Acıkara, Foçakarası, Papazkarası, Tilki Kuyruğu, Merzifon Karası, Adakarası, Urla Karası, Gaydura, Çalkarası, Karalahna, Kuntra (Karasakız)

*(White)* - Sultaniye, Bornova Misketi, Emir, Narince, Hasandede, Vasilaki, Çavuş

*Local varieties such as Kalecik Karası, Çalkarası, and Papazkarası are used to make rosé wine.

## Production Zones

### Thrace and Marmara

Çorlu, Tekirdağ, Kumbağ, Gaziköy, Hoşköy, Mürefte, Şarköy, Kavakköy, Gelibolu, Eceabat, Büyükkarıştıran, Lüleburgaz, Kırklareli, Mudanya, Adapazarı, Uzunköprü

### Aegean Region

İzmir, Foça, Manisa, Urla, Çeşme, Denizli (Pamukkale), Seferihisar, Torbalı, Şirince, Aydın, Muğla

### Central Black Sea Region

Tokat

### Central Anatolia

Kalecik (Ankara), Nevşehir (Cappadocia), Kayseri, Kırıkkale, Kırşehir, Çorum, Merzifon

### Eastern Anatolia

Elazığ, Diyarbakır, Malatya, Gaziantep

### Islands

Bozcaada, Avşa Adası, Gökçeada

### Mediterranean Region

Elmalı

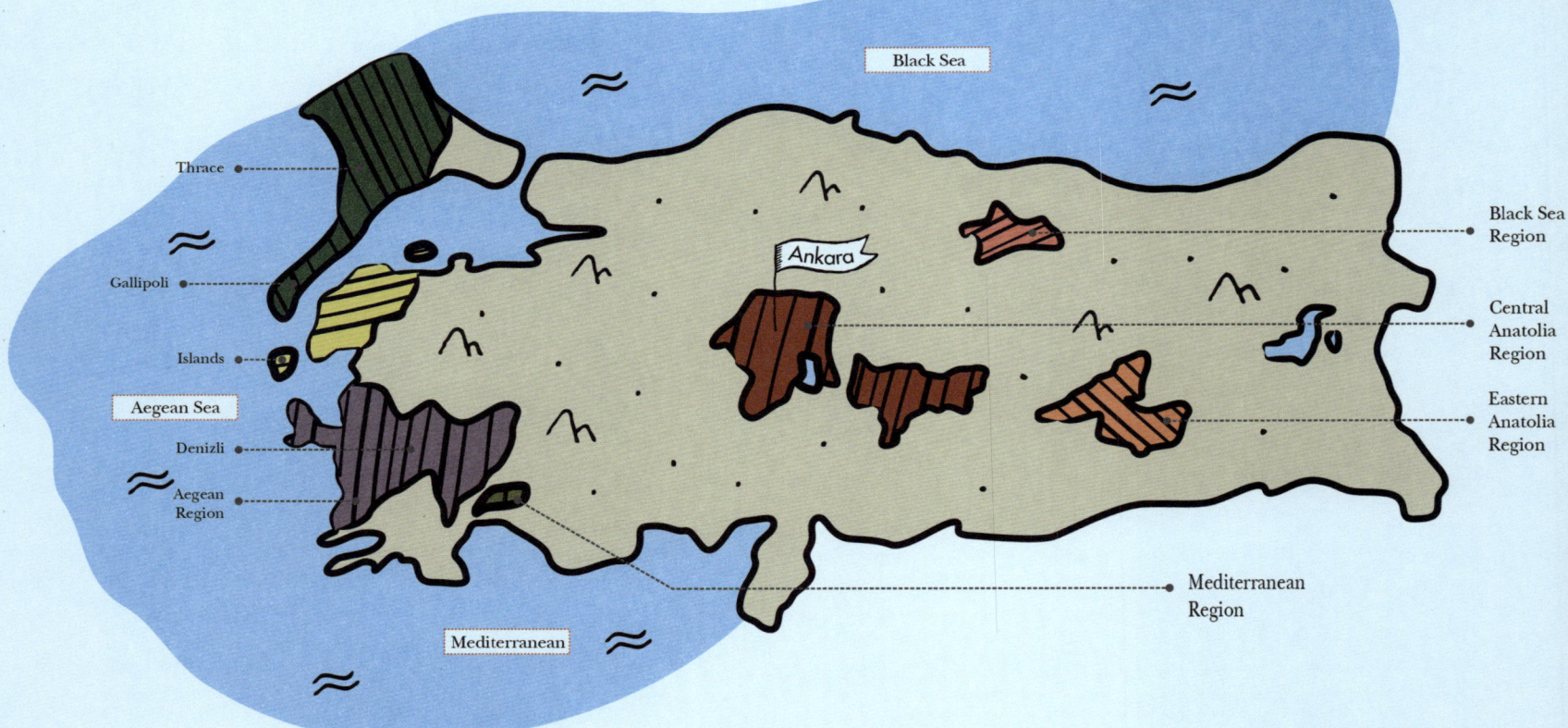

Kalecik Karası Wines (Ankara), Boğazkere Wines (Diyarbakır), Denizli Wines, and Urla Wines (Urla Karası) are wines that have been geographically registered exclusively in Türkiye and are protected by the Turkish Patent and Trademark Office (TÜRKPATENT). As of now, no geographical indication registration has been obtained for wines from Türkiye within the European Union. However, some wines that are geographically registered in Türkiye have the potential to receive geographical indication protection in the EU. The registration of Turkish wines by international institutions will also contribute to their promotion in the international market.

# Turkish Wine Reloaded

**Göknur Gündoğan,** *PhD, Author, Wine Expert*

From a geographical perspective, Türkiye forms a natural bridge between Europe, Asia and Africa. It could be said that it is an enormous peninsula, extending over 783,562 km² forming the westernmost point of Asia. Today, nearly 550,000 hectares of cultivated vines spread across the Turkish landscape. As one of the largest producers of table grapes, alongside France, Italy and Spain, Türkiye is ranked fifth in the world in terms of total area dedicated to vines, but unfortunately, only a small percentage of its production is assigned to winemaking.

In 2022 nearly 80 million litres of wine was produced. According to the International Organization of Vine and Wine (OIV), Türkiye contributes 0.05% of the world's wine production and represents just 0.06% of global wine consumption. Following my meetings with the historian and guide Murat Yankı, an eminent wine enthusiast, together we examined the historical journey of the vine in Türkiye. Murat developed the first historical map of 'sites' where wine was once produced in Türkiye. Following excavations in the 2010s, these count to around fifty today.

The geographical region covering these archaeological sites is interesting in the context of the history of the vine worldwide; according to recent research, findings show traces of the cultivated vine (i.e. Vitis vinifera L.) and the wild vine (Vitis sylvestris) dating back to 6,000 BC.

> **Anatolia is currently considered to be one of the original areas of production of our favourite plant.**

Specialist researchers of the 20th century including Billiard, Lutz, Levadoux, Negrul, Hyams and Johnson, also underline the importance of the terroirs between the Black Sea and the Caspian Sea (encompassing Türkiye, Georgia, Armenia, Azerbaijan, Iran, Iraq). Northern Mesopotamia, specifically the rivers of Euphrates and Tigris, which is today South-Eastern Anatolia in Türkiye is a unique region considered to be the heart of viticulture and the cradle of several civilizations, namely the Sumerians, Akkadians, Assyrians, Babylonians as well as the Hittites. (Unwin, 1996)

Traces (such as buried seeds) of one of the oldest wild vines (Vitis sylvestris) have been found in Nevali Çori near the Turkish city of Urfa, dating back 8,400 years. Analyses carried out on these Vitis sylvestris seeds (Arroyo-Garcia et al., 2006), support the previous thesis of Negrul (in 1938) indicating the Anatolian peninsula and the Transcaucasian region as the richest "centres of biodiversity" for Vitis Vinifera. The 2012 article titled; "History of Wine: Southeast Türkiye is said to be the cradle of the vine" which appeared in the first and one of the most influential magazines on viticulture in the world, "La Revue du vin de France" (LARVF) also supports a similar statement.

We have seen that it is likely that the origins of the vine go back to these distinct geographical regions with research focused on several areas including Georgia, Mesopotamia and Anatolia. Of course, this is not a race for who can claim the origin of the vine, considering each year new scientific research moves the original production area to another city in the region. However, it is important to underline that Anatolia is currently considered to be one of the original areas of production of our favourite plant.

The LARVF article was led by Swiss botanist and world-leading specialist on the origin and parentage of grape varieties, José Vouillamoz, who was one of three authors of the reference book "Wine Grapes" (Ed. Penguin Group, 2012) alongside two Masters of Wine; Jancis Robinson and Julia Harding. Joined by molecular biology specialist Patrick McGovern, they observed the DNA of domestic and wild vines around the world. In his study, Vouillamoz reports; "We started by collecting samples from vines in what I call the Near East, i.e. Anatolia, Armenia and Georgia, to determine where the wild grape was, genetically speaking, the closest to the cultivated grape varieties. It turned out to be Southeastern Anatolia." The Swiss scientist adds that; "We therefore put forward the hypothesis that it is most likely at this place that the vine was domesticated for the first time". This thesis is supported by laboratory work carried out at the University of Pennsylvania by Patrick McGovern. Analyses of residues of liquids collected on ancient boats have also concluded that today's grands crus have an Anatolian origin.

Anatolia is at the heart of the famous "croissant fertile" (Mesopotamia, a region covering today's Türkiye, Iraq and Syria), and according to research by Swiss scientists, one grape variety from the area is thought to be the parent of 80 European varieties, including Chardonnay, Gamay and Riesling. This is the White Gouais (Gouais Blanc), consequently baptized as the "grape casanova".

> **Vinolus, one of the leading boutique wine brands in Türkiye, is a unique success story penned by a contemporary Turkish woman from Kayseri in Cappadocia.**

In summary, over more than 8,000 years of viticultural history, the first domesticated vines appeared between 8,500 and 5,000 BC. Research has uncovered nearly 1,000 local grape varieties that are unique to the Anatolian Peninsula. We must dwell for a moment on the Hittite Empire, and its highly prosperous viticulture production across the Mediterranean basin. From the second half of the 17th century BC, the kings of the Hittites built one of the most powerful kingdoms in

the Middle East, dominating Anatolia until around 1200 BC. Various archaeological objects relating to viticulture in Anatolia have been uncovered on Hittite sites. The great Hittite Empire, ignored by historians until the beginning of the 20th century, is an important and influential civilization for the wine world. This empire, which reached its peak between 1,450 and 1,200 BC, left behind thousands of well-preserved written tablets testifying to its incredible wine culture. For example, the Hittites appear to be the first to have created wine laws. Hundreds of registered laws in fact! It is remarkable to see details on the tablets referring to their wine production, such as "the stakes" or descriptions and classifications of specific plots such as; "vineyards belonging to public" or "vineyards belonging to temples".

Finally, it is worth noting that a city near Antalya in southern Türkiye was once called Wiyanawanda (Oinoanda) by the Hittites, which meant "the city of wine."

In the 15th century the rise of the Muslim Ottomans changed everything and most of Anatolia became Islamised. This period is also marked by the conquest of Constantinople and the end of the Byzantine Empire in 1453.

During the period of the Ottoman Empire, wine was consumed primarily by the non-Muslim population, and in secret in Greek taverns in cities such as Istanbul and Izmir by a small number of Ottomans. It is known in Ottoman history that there were sultans who liked to drink wine, however, archival documents proving this are relatively rare. It's worth recalling the famous story of "Château Carbonnieux" and the Benedictine monks who were specialists in commerce. These monks managed to sell their white wines to the Ottoman Palace in the 18th century during the reign of Sultan Abdülhamid I., explaining to him that "it was indeed pure mineral water from Carbonnieux". The Ottoman Sultan was probably no fool but happily ignored this fact by asking his followers in this way; "If French mineral waters are so good, why do these people bother to make wine?".

The phylloxera crisis that destroyed much of Europe's vineyards in the 19th century had an unforeseen consequence: it heralded a wave of wine exports from the Ottoman Empire to countries across the continent, including France, Spain and Italy. History also makes note of French wine houses attempting to plant vines in Thrace. In 1904, the Ottoman export of wine to Europe amounted to 340 million litres. Almost four times that of today's total production!

The paradoxes and hypocrisies regarding the consumption of wine only ended in the early 20th century. The modern Turkish Republic opened a new era for the wine industry. When Mustafa Kemal Atatürk came into power in 1923, he abolished the Empire as well as the Sharia from 1920. He closed the religious courts, gave women the right to vote, and alcohol consumption was made legal, encouraging the planting of vineyards, a symbol of secularism and a potential economic resource for the new Türkiye. Today, Turks continue to be great consumers of raisins, vinegar, molasses and pickles of which the raw material are grapes. This partly explains the huge area of vines that were protected across Türkiye.

Following the Greco-Turkish War (1919-1922), and the subsequent Treaty of Lausanne, Greece and Türkiye carried out a population exchange in 1923. As one of the first large-scale compulsory population transfers based on ethnicity and religion, it profoundly affected both nations. Anatolian Greeks were sent to Greece, which was bad news for wine, as it was the Greek population who maintained the vineyards and understood the traditional art of Anatolian viticulture. Atatürk, seeing that the wine industry was in decline, summoned specialists from Bordeaux in 1926 to help solve the problem. The Turkish state consequently supported and funded wine production, and large

*e famous ceramic cchus mask of Siena: cchus (Dionysos) has ong historical and tural ties to Anatolia rough mythological gins, religious practices, iculture, and artistic presentations, strating the region's nificant role in the cient worship and ebration of the god of ne.*

producers such as "Doluca" and "Kavaklıdere" were established (in 1929). In addition, international grape varieties were planted; with a focus on Semillon, Gamay, Carignan and Cinsault.

It is still thanks to Atatürk that the secular State revived a wine tradition that dates back several millennia, and as a young republic, a large wine research centre was founded in Ankara in 1929. This interest in wine continued through to 1943 with the second President of the Republic, Ismet Inönü, who initiated the establishment of several wine research centres in selected production areas, with French specialists invited to work alongside young Turkish researchers.

Unfortunately, this brilliant initiative fell into oblivion in the 1950s, at the same time as the closure of the "Village Institutes" (Köy Enstitüleri) which trained young farmers and winegrowers in their villages of origin. The right-wing political party that took power (The Democratic Party) took the decision to close these innovative centres and institutes under the pretext of various socio-political reasons.

The current Turkish wine market is made up of large producers each producing several million litres every year as well as small and medium-sized houses. The latter produce several styles of wines, ranging from small quantities of fine nectars to larger quantities intended for daily consumption. Since the end of the monopoly in 2003, several small wineries have developed. Before this time, although a few independent private producers existed, TEKEL (which means monopoly in the Turkish language) was "the" main state structure regulating and controlling the market for alcoholic beverages and tobacco. TEKEL was privatised and its name changed to "MEY." In 2006 MEY was sold to an American group, TPG Capital; and then in 2011, MEY was bought by the English multinational, Diageo. Diageo has since modernized its production infrastructure and wineries, creating a unique and prestigious brand for its wines, the "Kayra" brand which currently produces 11 million

> Oluş focused on reviving the 2000-acre farm inherited from her ancestors, engaging in organic agriculture with local seeds.

litres of wine per year, corresponding to one seventh of the country's annual production.

Although considerable progress has been made to viticultural practices in the 21st century, much of Türkiye's vineyards continue to feature traditional "gobelet trained" vines, which are not conducive to mechanization. Production costs remain high, making it difficult to market and promote wines at an international level, whilst bulk wines produced by large producers are intended for specific consumers, as found in the popular tourist spots around the country's Mediterranean coast.

Let's not forget that only 2% to 5% of the production of fresh grapes is destined for winemaking in Türkiye; and contrary to the average annual consumption per person in Europe, Türkiye's national wine consumption remains low with an annual average not exceeding one litre per person.

Finally, we would like to highlight some of the larger producers; Kayra, Doluca, Kavaklıdere, Pamukkale and Sevilen.

Among the medium and small producers we can also note; Arcadia Vineyards, Arda, Asmadan, Akın Gürbüz, Asarcık, Ayda Winery, Barbare, Barel, Corvus, Chamlıja, Chateau Kalpak, Chateau Nuzun, Çamlıbağ, Edrine, Gordias, Kastro Tireli, Gelveri, Kocabağ, Küp, Kuzeybağ, Kuzubağ, LA, Likya, Maadra, Melen, Mesashuna, Urla, Nif, Öküzgözü Şarapçılık, Etruscan, Selendi, Selefkia, Sobran, Suvla, Şatomet, Talay, Tomurcukbağ, Usca, Urlice, Vinolus, Yedi Bilgiler, Umurbey, Paşaeli, Prodom, Tafali, Vinkara, Yükseltan, Heraki, Hus, Lermonos, Ni&Ce Bağları, Turasan and Yanık Ülke.

Vinolus, one of the leading boutique wine brands in Türkiye, is a unique success story, penned by a contemporary Turkish woman from Kayseri in Cappadocia. Thanks so much, dear Oluş.

*For more detailed information: Gündoğan, Göknur – Yankı, Murat: Oenotourism Guide to Turkey. 2021 Istanbul (ISBN 978-625-449-424-6)*

# Arif Molu
## 1901-1973

# The Molu Family and Oluş

Oluş is part of the Molu family, one of the oldest and most prominent families in Kayseri. It is rumoured that the family originates from the Turkish Gökoğuzlar tribe, and the abundance of blue-eyed individuals within the family is evidence of this. While some family members claim that their roots trace back to the Dulkadıroğulları Principality in Eastern Anatolia, established after the Seljuk period (from the 11$^{th}$ to 13$^{th}$ centuries AD), there are no written records supporting this claim. The first written source related to the family dates back five hundred years.

It is right to say that the Molu family has owned vast swaths of land for centuries. In the traditional land management systems of the Seljuk and Ottoman Empires, such large estates were granted to commanders who demonstrated bravery in wars, these grants were known as Timar (or vassalage), and these commanders were referred to as Bey or Ağa (landlord). As landlords, they paid taxes to the state in exchange for their allocated property and would commit to join battles with a certain number of soldiers if necessary. For instance, it is known that Yavuz Sultan Selim's Kayseri Bey, Üveyis Bey, who participated in the Çaldıran Campaign (in 1514) and was martyred in the battle, belonged to the Molu family, according to the book "Tâcü't Tevârih" from about five centuries ago.

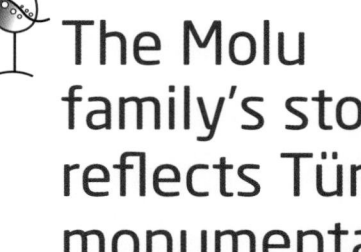

**The Molu family's story reflects Türkiye's monumental transformation over the past century.**

Moving forward, the Molu family's oldest recorded ancestors are Hüseyin Ağa, who lived in the second half of the seventeenth century, and his son Mustafa Ağa, who passed away in 1721, ten generations ago. The most well-known forebear is Molu'lu Arif Ağa, who lived in the nineteenth century, the great-great-grandfather of Oluş Molu.

Arif Ağa resided in the village of Molu, located approximately 20 kilometres from Kayseri, surrounded by lands inherited within the

**Mehmet Şahin,** *President of Erciyes University a.d.*

*...if Molu's sons, Sait, Faruk, Metin and Mustafa Molu. Oluş's father, Faruk Molu, through his role in ... State Plannning Organisation, helped to shape and influence Türkiye's economic development strategies.*

family. During his time, the traditional land system of the Ottoman Empire underwent a transformation, transitioning to a more capitalist system of property ownership during the the Republican Era. Arif Ağa engaged in farming and animal husbandry, leading flocks of sheep to distant corners of the Ottoman Empire, such as Egypt. His son Mustafa Ağa, who lived during the decline of the Ottoman Empire in the late nineteenth and early twentieth centuries, unfortunately struggled to maintain the integrity of the Molu family's lands, which went into decline.

Following the passing of Mustafa Ağa in 1922, his son Arif Molu became the patriarch of the Molu family. Born in 1901, Arif completed middle school and, during World War I began working in the glassware business alongside his brother-in-law, Alim Bey while managing the farm. This early exposure to a different perspective on business life, beyond traditional farming, provided Arif with a fresh, new outlook; a philosophy that is today carried on by Oluş with her innovative approach to farming.

Arif had four sons, all of whom he sent to Germany for education from 1951. Oluş's father, Faruk Molu, graduated from Istanbul University's Law Faculty and then studied economics in Germany, where he married Marianna Hanım in Kiel. Their first child, Oluş, was born in Germany.

Oluş graduated from the Biochemistry Department of Hacettepe University in Ankara and, unlike other family members who went into commerce, she focused on reviving the 2000-acre farm inherited from her ancestors, engaging in organic agriculture cultivating indigenous seeds and plants, and educating the public, especially the youth, in sustainable farming practice.

The story of the Molu family's transition from land owners to traders, then to railway subcontracting, railway contracting, factory owners and agriculture-based industrial production, mirrors and reflects Türkiye's monumental transformation over the past century.

# VINOLUS by José

Cultivating grapes to produce wine is an exciting profession, and coming from Spain to Türkiye to create wine was not a difficult decision; it was rather a culmination of circumstances, created from a passion for travel and a desire to expand my viticulture and viniculture experience and expertise across several countries. Oluş and her winery were two of the key motives that enticed me to come to Türkiye.

When I first met Oluş, with the aim to join her vineyard team, she had very precise ideas on what she wanted to achieve with her wines - wines that reflect the vineyard and the grape variety alongside the terroir of Cappadocia. An ambitious and challenging project given the social considerations of the region and the lack of modern technological standards.

Once you are in the country, it doesn't take long to realise how diverse Turkish viticulture is - a fact often overlooked by the local people. More and more, it feels as though the appreciation of how unique this wine region is slowly being lost. Today, Türkiye is the fifth largest country in the world in terms of total vineyard area, and the impact of a centuries-old wine culture on its various civilisations and inhabitants has been significant. As a wine region, the country is home to the largest and most varied number of indigenous grape varieties on the planet.

> We are making wines with a great sense of place, expressing the characteristics of the 'terroir' that make them unique wines in the world.

Although Anatolia has always had a wine growing tradition, its wine culture has diminished in more recent times. Türkiye is a cosmopolitan country yet is also one where it can be difficult to find a middle ground – it is a country of extremes. This concept is also widely experienced in the world of Turkish wine, where it is easy to find the greatest wine enthusiasts alongside the staunchest detractors who believe that fermenting grape juice into wine is a sin. This latter belief is more

**José Hernández,** *Vinolus Oenologist Co-owner of Heraki Wines in Türkiye*

*...ş, José, and İnanç ...efing international ...mmeliers at the ...logna Slow Wine Fair ...24, one of the most ...ortant events in the ...e industry's calendar.*

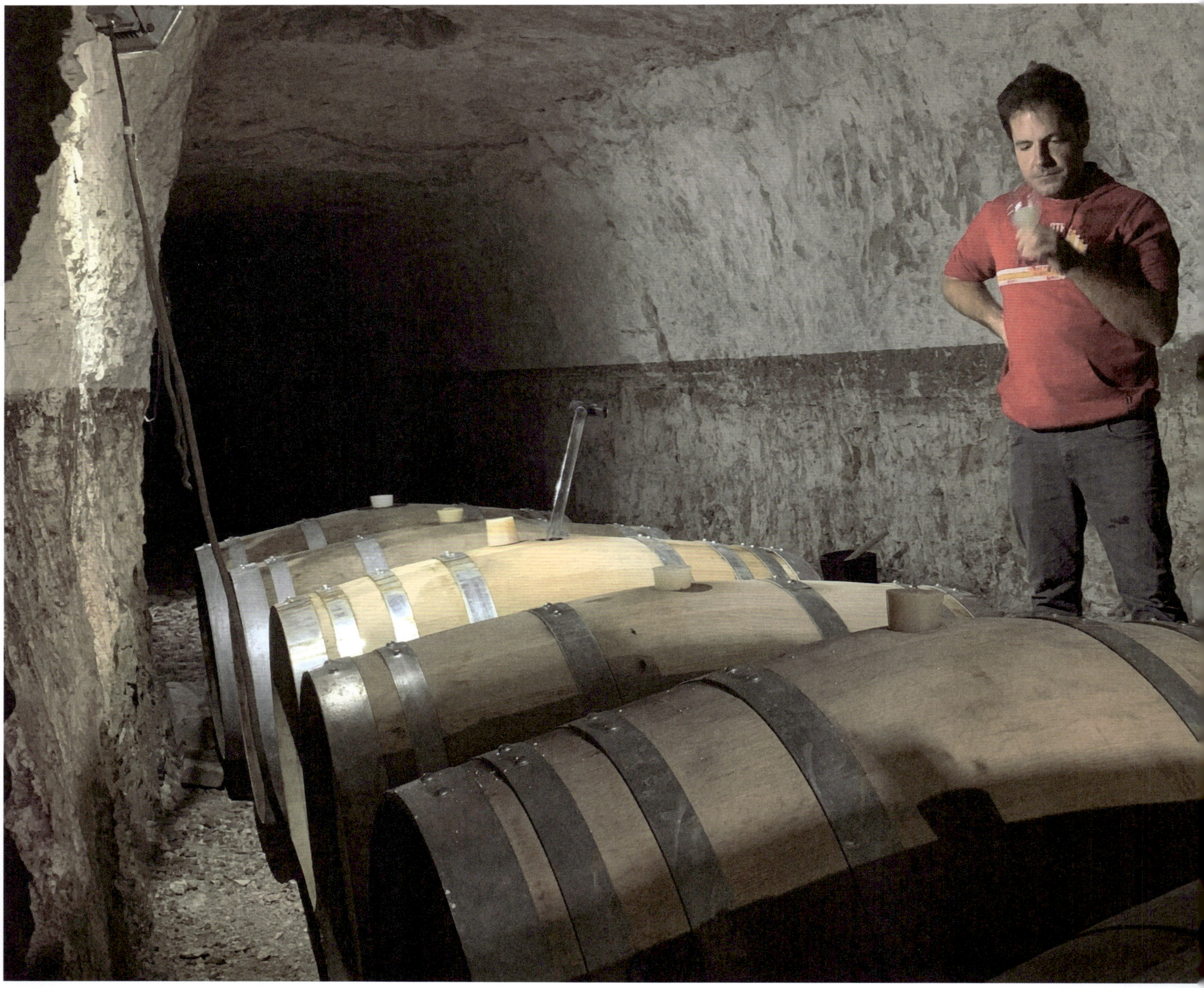

*They wonder how this year's wine turned out? Oluş and José hard at work.*

common in the interior and the east of the country, which is where Oluş has established her oasis of oenological autonomy. With a distinct awareness and understanding of the potential of the region's volcanic ash and calcareous soils, her wines are bestowed with a unique identity and character reflecting this special terroir.

The mountainous area of Kayseri is also renowned for its extreme continental climate, where vines are one of the few crops that can survive the extremely cold winters and minimal precipitation. With all of these challenges, Oluş has managed to add value and a unique style to her family's lands and vineyards. Making wine in Türkiye is like taking a leap into the void, but doing so in a place like Kayseri is like jumping out of a 'plane without a parachute. One must have immense resilience, passion, and a capacity for struggle and hard work - qualities that Oluş has in abundance.

As mentioned, cultivating vines in Cappadocia is not an easy task. Within the bureaucratic complexities of producing wines in the interior of Anatolia, Oluş has also been revolutionary in how she grows and produces her wines; she is one of the first to create organic wines in Türkiye ensuring everything she does comes with the utmost respect for the environment and the land's natural resources.

As a result of this effort and teamwork, we are able to produce premium wines to the highest international standards. At Vinolus, we cultivate local varieties such as Narince from white grapes and Kalecik Karasi from black grapes, supporting and adding value to the local biodiversity. We also produce wines from a number of internationally-recognised varieties that add diversity, support soil health and create interest in the region in terms of tourism and consumption on a national and international level. In short, we make wines with a wonderful sense of place, expressing the characteristics of the "terroir"; curating wines that are truly unique on a global level.

Just as people come to Cappadocia from all corners of the world to discover its history and landscapes, the wines of Vinolus are another photograph of Cappadocia - a photograph in a glass of wine of the grape varieties we nurture and the soils where our vines are cultivated.

If you have a passion for wine, these are wines you must try.

**SUNOLUS BAĞEVİ**
SUNOLUS VINEYARD HOUSE

## Chef JORG ZUPAN

*Venison, kohlrabi, coriander, chili*
*Rose*

*Confited mushrooms, yeast crackers, lichens, mushroom "tea"*
*Chardonnay*

*Beetroot in chicken fat, crispy chicken skin, jus, kale*
*Kalecik Karası*

*Grilled cabbage steamed with buttermilk, sumac,*
*salsa verde from radish leaves, roasted cabbage dutch sauce*
*Syrah*

*Pigeon, quince, glazed chestnut, chestnut puree and pigeon bone*
*and Barbera wine miso sauce*
*Blend*

*Tangerines, goat cheese, corn*

*Miso, chocolate, pear, coffee caramel, pumpkin oil*
*Liquor*

At the gastrodiplomacy evening jointly organised by JRE and Oluş, Jorg Zupan presented a Slovenian cuisine menu paired with Vinolus wines. This event was held on the occasion of Slovenia's EU Council Presidency.

# My Experience with Vinolus in Cappadocia: A Culinary Journey of Flavours

**Jorg Zupan,** *Michelin Star Chef & JRE Member Chef*

In the fascinating world of gastronomy, food and wine hold a special place, intertwining culture, history, and tradition. In this personal culinary journey, I embark on a very special adventure of exploration inspired by Oluş Molu. It was because of Oluş that I discovered the unique flavours of Turkish wines and their intriguing connection to my native Slovenian cuisine. As I dived into Türkiye's rich wine tapestry with Vinolus, within the framework of Slovenia's culinary culture, it is the influence of the Ottoman Empire on Balkan cooking traditions that was the most profound for me.

### Vinolus Wines: A Symphony of Tastes

Türkiye, a land steeped in history and blessed with a diverse variety of landscapes, has been home to vineyards since ancient times. Turkish wines boast a rich heritage that date back thousands of years, making viticulture an important part of the country's cultural identity. With over 1,400 indigenous grape varieties, the wines of Türkiye offer a captivating symphony of tastes, each reflecting the unique terroir of its respective region.

> Turkish wines are a true revelation for the palate.

The winemaking traditions in Türkiye are deeply intertwined with local customs and practices, making it a wonderful experience to sample and taste the various indigenous varietals. From the crisp and refreshing whites of the Aegean coast to the bold and full-bodied reds from Thrace and Cappadocia, Turkish wines are a true revelation for the palate.

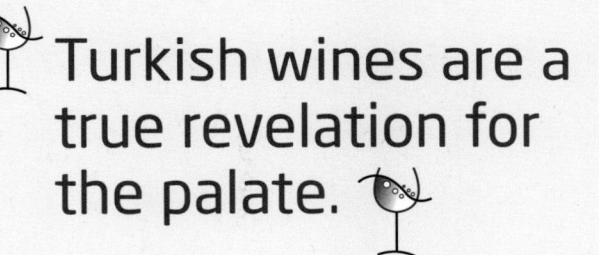

It was a unique experience for me to visit Oluş' vineyard in Cappadocia, a region rich in distinct geographical features and cultural characteristics. It was an honour for me to present my Slovenian cuisine in Türkiye paired with Turkish wine. It was here that I had the opportunity to match Vinolus with a few of my Slovenian-inspired dishes.

At the heart of Europe lies my home, Slovenia, a country known for its breathtaking landscapes and culinary scene that celebrates fresh, seasonal ingredients. Slovenian cuisine is a harmonious blend of flavours, heavily influenced by neighbouring countries and their

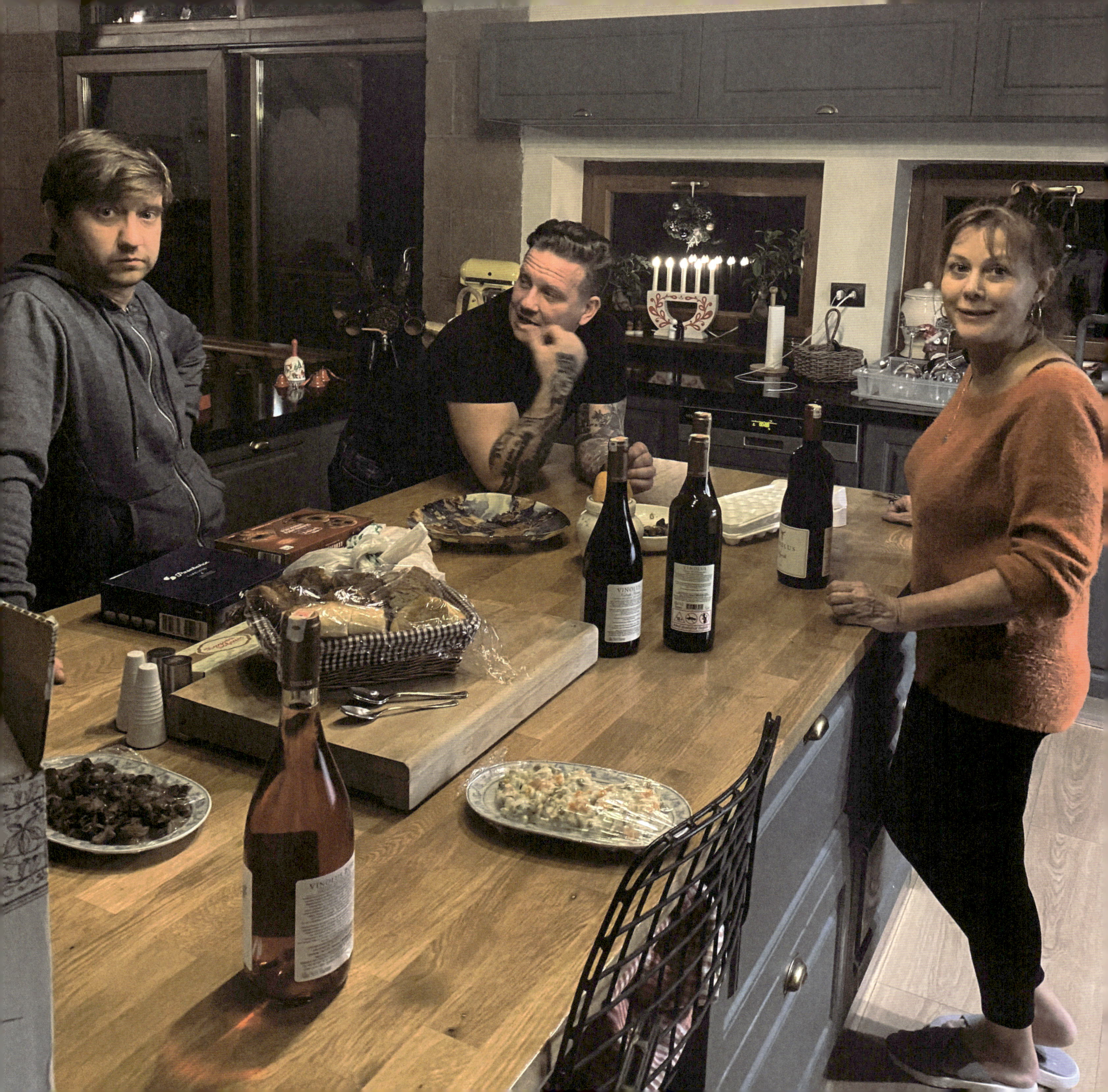
VINOLUS

historical connections. Due to Slovenia's geographical position, its culinary ethos is influenced by the cuisine of the Alps, the Mediterranean, and the Pannonian Plain.

Traditional Slovenian dishes are crafted with love and pride, with a focus on preserving age-old recipes. From hearty stews to delicate pastries, Slovenian cuisine promises to enchant even the most discerning food enthusiasts.

As a Slovenian Chef, I was fascinated to dive deeper into the wine culture of Türkiye, and through this I uncovered the intriguing influence of the Ottoman Empire on Balkan cooking traditions. The Ottomans left an indelible mark on the culinary landscape of southeastern Europe, introducing new ingredients, spices, and cooking techniques.

During the Ottoman reign, cultural exchanges between Türkiye and Slovenia resulted in a culinary fusion that continues today. Reflecting the enduring legacy of this historical connection, traditional Slovenian dishes often feature flavours that can be traced back to the Ottomans, embracing Turkish spices, such as Burek, Baklava and Štruklji, paprika, cinnamon and cumin; along with specialties such as rolled dough filled with Turkish Sarma (stuffed grape leaves), Mantı (dumplings), or Polnjene Paprike (stuffed vegetables).

With an eye for detail and an adventurous palate, I was keen to discover what makes Turkish wines so distinctive. As I immersed myself in the world of Turkish viticulture, I discovered the warm hospitality of the locals, who take immense pride in sharing their wine traditions complemented by their diverse range of wines, which truly captivated my senses.

I noted how Oluş skilfully blends traditional methods with modern techniques, producing wines that are both innovative and true to their roots. From vibrant rosés to rich reds, the wine portfolio of Vinolus offers an enticing selection that pairs beautifully with a variety of dishes.

Turkish wines matched with regional dishes of Cappadocia, for example Meze, Çökelekli Börek (a type of savoury pastry) and stuffed grape leaves, create a harmonious masterpiece of flavours, exemplifying the connection between wine and food in Turkish society.

To conclude, through my personal culinary lens, I have been fortunate to embark on a fascinating journey uniting the wine culture of Türkiye with Slovenian cuisine. It was through the discovery of the distinctive flavours of Turkish wines that I came to acknowledge how centuries of history and tradition have shaped Türkiye's viticulture.

The intriguing interplay between Turkish wines and Slovenian dishes is a testament to the shared heritage of the Balkans, with the Ottoman Empire's influence leaving a lasting impression on both cultures. This culinary journey has undoubtedly deepened my appreciation for the artistry and harmony that exist between food, wine, and culture.

Thank you, Oluş.

> **Through the discovery of the distinctive flavours of Turkish wines, I came to acknowledge how centuries of history and tradition have shaped Türkiye's viticulture.**

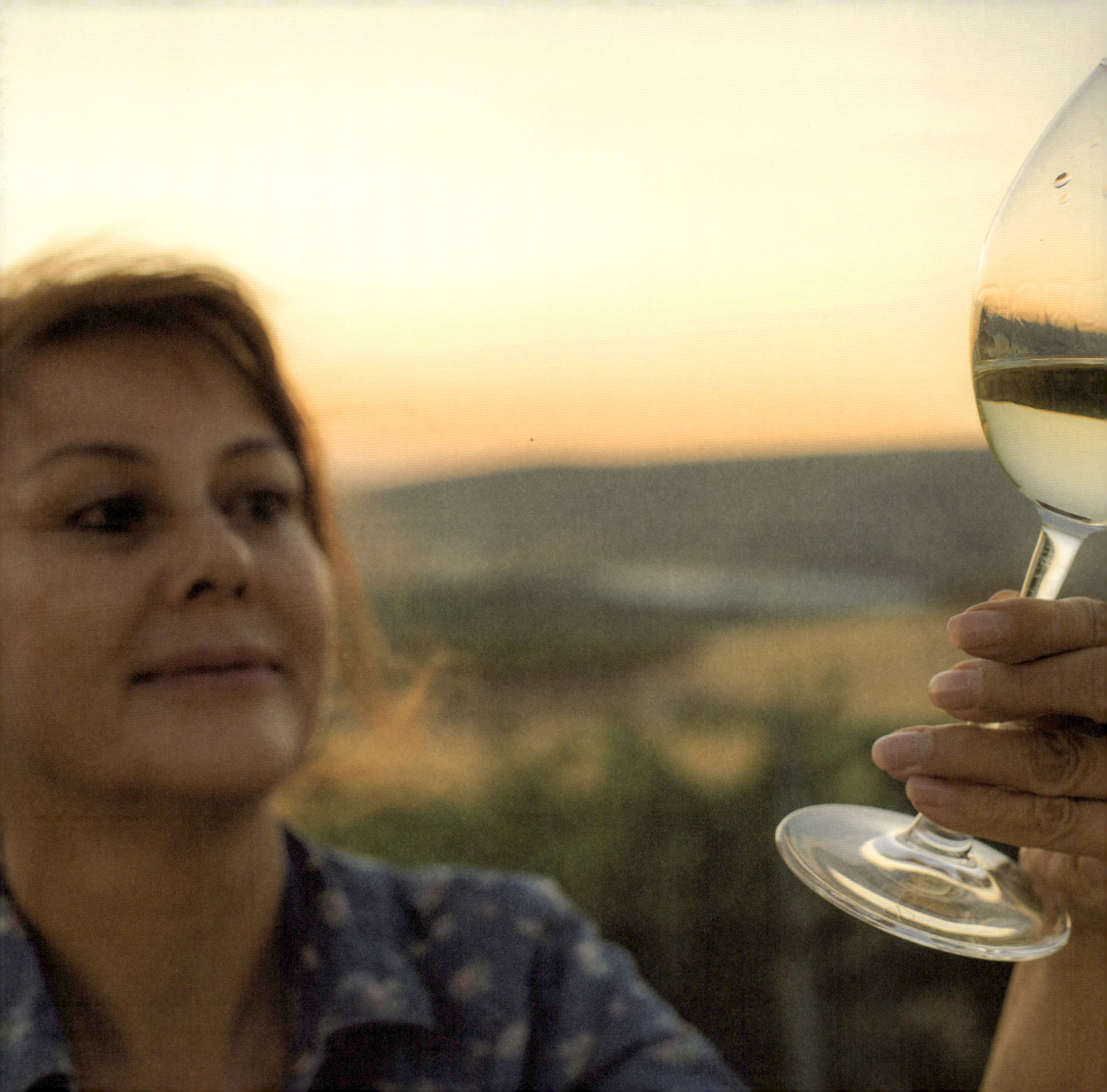

# The Productive and Sustainable World of my Sister, Oluş

**Azra Seyok**, *Chairwoman of the Board of Directors, Karsu Textile*

Oluş is a passionate advocate for our wine culture, with nature at the heart of everything she does. Oluş is also an entrepreneur and an activist. In addition to her demanding and successful endeavours with wine, I'd like to focus on how my sister's passion for nature and agriculture interweaves with our family history.

Oluş's unique outlook on life, and how she determined her career path all started during our childhood, influenced by the wonderful times we spent at our grandfather's farm in Kayseri. Arif Molu, our grandfather, championed Atatürk's goals for Türkiye's development and achieved numerous successes in the early years of the Republic. Born in 1901 in Kayseri, our grandfather's various career highlights included working on the subcontracting of railway lines and construction of the Niğde Gebere Dam; with our grandfather pivoting into agriculture after WWII. Later on, in the 1950s, he played a major role in founding Kayseri's first sugar factory, followed by textile factories, and was the founder of the Karsu textile company. Renowned as a visionary and philanthropist, our grandfather believed in the power of education, establishing the first Imam-Hatip school and the Kayseri Islamic Institute, which later became part of Erciyes University.

> **Preventing the destruction of nature is key as it takes a long time to restore nature that is destroyed.**

When we were little, during his move into agriculture, our grandfather developed a farm and built a house for our family close to Kayseri. This small vineyard house, this home, was fairly modest; there was no electricity or water, we had to draw water from a well. Yet being on the farm for us was enchanting; with much of our childhood, especially in the summers, spent on the farm. What our vineyard house lacked in comfort, it made up for in joy, they were happy years, fully immersed and surrounded by nature. Back then, our childhood imaginations ran wild with ideas of turning the farm into a vast forest filled with animals. In fact, in the arid lands of Anatolia, where water is scarce, our grandfather must have performed miracles on his land; we felt as though we were in an oasis in the middle of the desert. Later on, our parents Marianne and Faruk Molu followed in our grandfather's footsteps, and their love for nature, trees, and animals is the greatest legacy that they gifted to us. Our mother bred the finest racehorses in Cappadocia, and in the 1980s, our father worked on reforestation, planting tens of thousands of black pine and cedar saplings on the land; a project and passion that Oluş continues today, planting saplings and ensuring the on-going health of the trees.

Oluş's career choice was partially influenced by these nature-filled childhood days at the farm, leading her to study biology at Hacettepe University in Ankara. After graduation, she worked as a research assistant and completed her master's thesis with the Zoology department. She then worked as an expert in biology for five years at the Special Environmental Protection Agency under the Ministry of Environment. At that time, there were 13 designated special environmental protection areas in Türkiye. My sister co-ordinated conservation projects and programmes aimed at identifying and protecting each area's flora and fauna.

Oluş is never idle; she has always worked and worked hard at that, with a special awareness and understanding of societal needs especially at a local level. In the early 2000s, she taught practical environmental education to school children and later served as a consultant on environmental education for children in the World Bank's project protecting biodiversity in Türkiye.

In 2007, Oluş decided to return from Ankara to Kayseri and share her knowledge with the farming community. By then, I believe her perspective on life had already started to take shape, focusing on how humanity's large-scale destruction and domination over nature needed to change. With this in mind, Oluş started with herself. Awareness led her to question her own mindset. She focused on environmentally-friendly and holistic production methods at the farm, pioneering the first organic production practices in Kayseri. When she applied for organic certification to the Provincial Directorate of Agriculture at that time, it was said that her application to for her farm to be recognised as organic was the first. By applying her scientific knowledge supported by a team of agricultural engineers, her organic approach successfully served as model for other farms and producers in the area. To create awareness and understanding of organic farming, she founded KAPTAR (Cappadocia Organic Producers Association). However, with limited producers in the region, her first task was to increase the number of farmers. With the support of the Kayseri Provincial Directorate of Agriculture, her work began, resulting in a huge upswing in the number of producers. Today, the region of Kayseri is home to extensive areas dedicated to organic production, alongside local organic markets established with the support of the Kayseri Municipality.

According to my sister, organic farming is not just a production method but a holistic perspective on life. While the term "growth" tends to be used to mean an increase in capacity, in organic farming, it indicates quality. It is about considering how organic farming benefits and transforms everything from the soil through to the people that consume the produce from that land. And practicing organic production means considering other factors, not just linked to the land, for example, transportation and logistics.

Oluş's aim with KAPTAR is to implement an organic production model across Kayseri. The association's goal is to prove that true, long term sustainability can be achieved by instigating this model. Within this, my sister prioritises education for the farming community, with noteworthy achievements, especially around social responsibility.

*Olus and her younger sister, Azra with their mother, Marianne, and father, Faruk standing proud in the background.*

Oluş approaches society and how we manage our daily lives from various angles, seeking out complementary solutions. In recent years, the general increase in cancer, obesity, and food allergies has made us question our dietary habits, perhaps encouraging us to take a pause and review our behaviours and outlook on life. Knowledge and technology will always play a role in our evolutionary development, however a lifestyle based on excessive consumption, where a sense of ownership turns into greed and selfishness, resulting in unhappiness has trapped humans in a vicious cycle. The only outcome of this cycle is disaster, with dire consequences for future generations. Yet, by changing our lifestyle, consumption, and dietary habits, by socialising the process, there is a chance we can leave nature as "NATURE" for generations to enjoy long after we have gone. In other words, this transformation rescue project, focussing on organic farming production methods can play a part in saving nature from destruction. As my sister Oluş Molu always says, "Preventing the destruction of nature is key, as it takes a long time to restore nature that is destroyed".

I wanted to highlight in this article that my sister is dedicated to sustainable, environmentally-friendly organic farming as a whole. You will be able to read about her valuable contributions to the wine industry in other sections of this book.

Our childhood imaginations ran wild with the idea of transforming the farm into a vast forest filled with animals.

*This must be love. Olus's parents.*

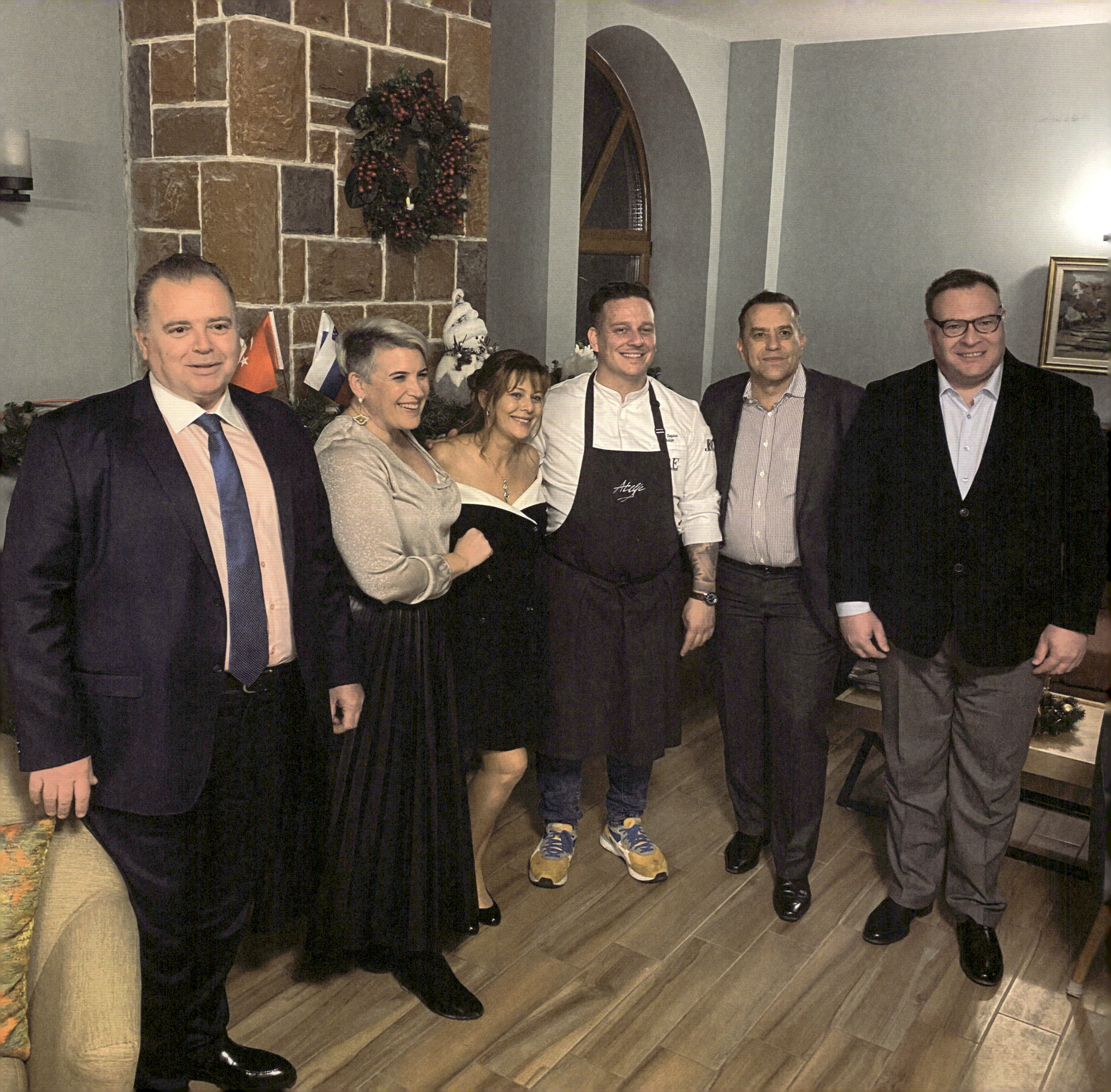

# Gastro-diplomacy and Oluş

**Perisa Kastratovic,**
*State Secretary at the Ministry of Foreign Affairs of Montenegro and former Ambassador to Türkiye.*

At the invitation of Oluş Molu and Dr. İnanç Atılgan, together with fellow ambassadors of the Republic of Ireland, Sonia McGuinness and Republic of Croatia, Hrvoje Cvitanovic, I was a guest an event in December 2021 at Molu Farm in Kayseri. In the surroundings of the beautiful Sunolus Vineyard House, thanks to our hosts, Oluş and the Ambassador of the Republic of Slovenia, Primoz Seligo, we had the opportunity to enjoy Vinolus wines, accompanied by dishes prepared by the renowned Slovenian Michelin-starred chef, Jorg Zupan. Bearing in mind that the event was attended by numerous guests from the social and political community of Kayseri, as well as representatives of the media, this was a very unique event - the best possible gastronomic presentation of the Republic of Türkiye and the Republic of Slovenia. All of us that were present enjoyed an extraordinary demonstration and example of Gastrodiplomacy.

> **Gastrodiplomacy is predicated on the notion that the easiest way to win hearts and minds is through the stomach.**

Like every profession transformed by modernisation, the art of diplomacy continually changes and transforms to keep up with the times. Interests are changeable bringing new areas of cooperation that may not have previously been considered. Diplomacy is becoming more and more complex and multifaceted, covering different aspects of life and using modern techniques like Gastrodiplomacy. Today, there is almost no reputable textbook that does not treat, or teach, different methods of diplomatic protocol such as economic diplomacy, cultural cooperation and other ways in which a country can be presented in its best light. A special place belongs to Gastrodiplomacy, especially when we take into account that gastronomy is increasingly used as a way to create and forge diplomatic relationships, playing an integral role in cross-cultural initiatives. We use national cuisine and culinary skills to present our country to others in an innovative yet modest way. The modern

*E. Perisa Kastratovic (far right), Slovenian Ambassador E. Primoz Seligo, chef Jorg Zupan, Oluş, Irish Ambassador E. Sonya Mc Guinness, and Croatian Ambassador E. Hrvoje Cvitanovic.*

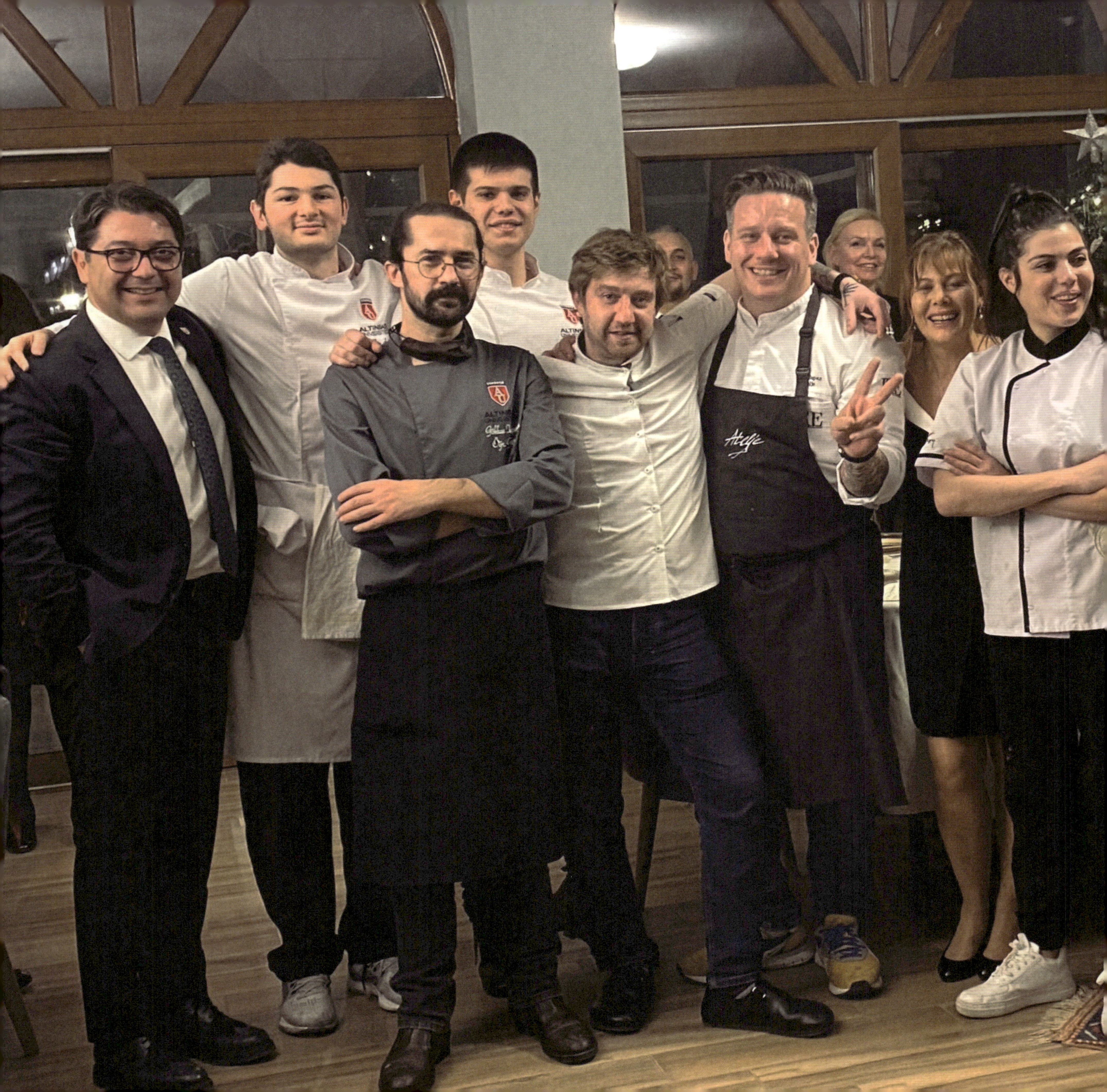

> Oluş as our host provided an inspirational example of Gastrodiplomacy, representing family tradition and Turkish hospitality.

*A proud moment. The menu was fantastic. From left to right: İnanç Atilgan, "future Michelin star" candidate Chef Gökhan Taşpınar, Chef Volkan Aray, Chef Furkan Kılıç, Chef Blaž Češnovar, Star Chef Jorg Zupan, Her Excellency Madam Oluş, Ekin Karayalçın, Chef Sercan Azbaz, and Yasemin Altınyay.*

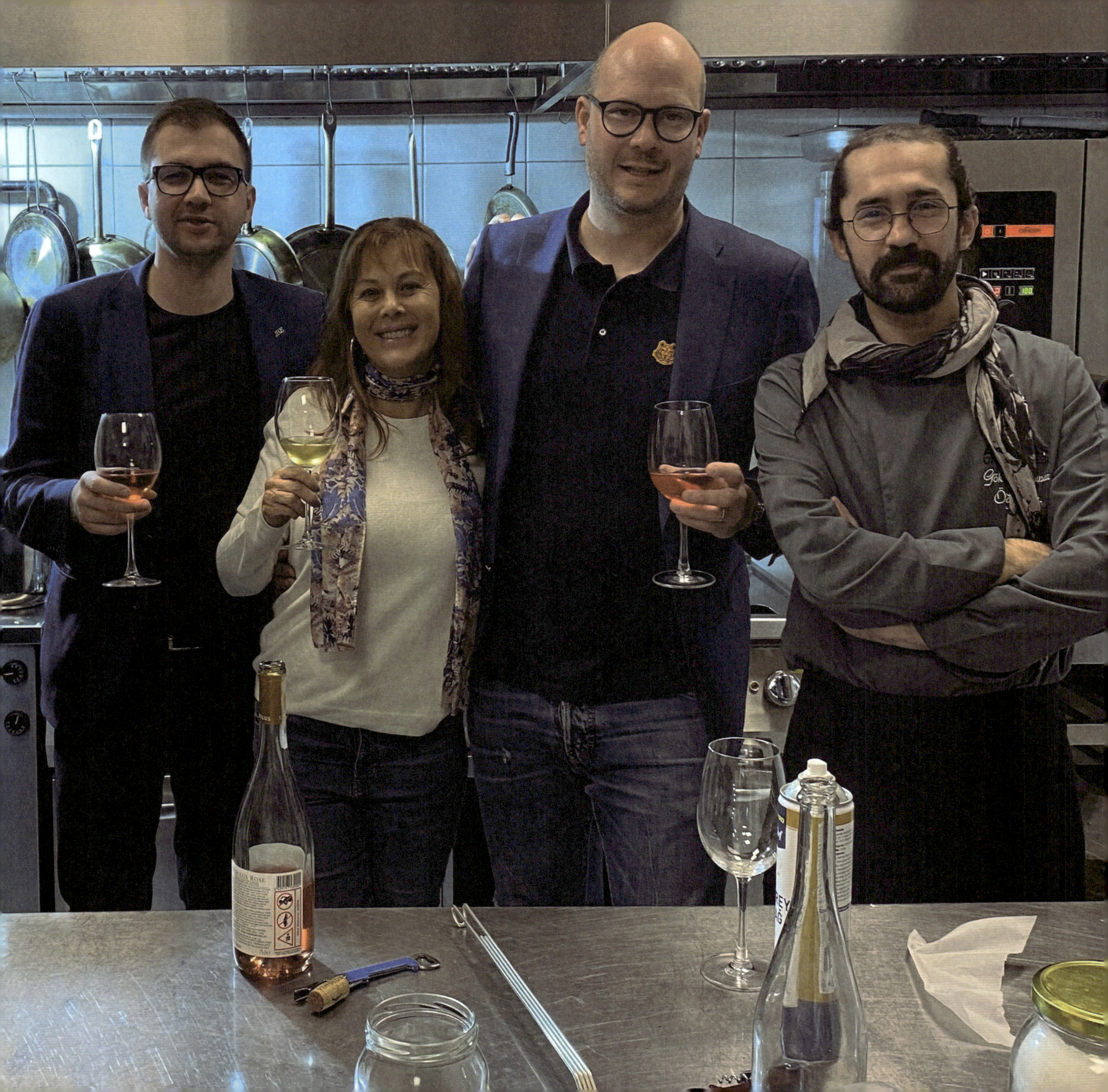

diplomatic service recognises the potential of gastronomy, which is an indispensable part of the cultural, geographical and historical heritage of any country. It is used as an accessible and highly effective way to create a positive impression about the people and the country. As Paul Rockewer, one of the public diplomacy scholars who popularised the term Gastrodiplomacy, writes: "Gastrodiplomacy is predicated on the notion that the easiest way to win hearts and minds is through the stomach." Even those who are not very informed or do not know much about other cultures, very easily associate certain dishes or drinks with specific regions and thus create a positive image of certain countries and their culture. Italian, French, Chinese, Mexican, as well as many other national cuisines have made an immense contribution to creating a positive image of those countries around the world. Considering I was representing my Republic in Türkiye, I can freely say that, in addition to the wide range of positive impressions that visitors to Türkiye take home with them, it's the variety of Turkish cuisine that is most fascinating. Turkish breakfast, Turkish delicacies, as well as Turkish coffee represent an indispensable part of the Turkish brand and positive associations with Türkiye, its culture and customs. Bearing in mind that Montenegro is a Mediterranean and Balkan country, as is my hosting country, and considering our shared history, there are many similarities when it comes to gastronomy and customs.

During my visit to Kayseri, thanks to the hospitality that Türkiye is renowned for, we had the opportunity to acquaint ourselves with Kayseri's historical sights, as well as its economic potential, especially regarding winter tourism.

The stories around family tradition and the history of the Molu family and their farm left a great impression on me. Oluş spoke with particular fondness about her family's multinationality and multiculturalism, mentioning her Turkish and German roots. With incredible patience, simplicity and finesse, she showed us laymen her vineyards, winery and cellars, where today - and this, after the tasting, I can freely say – some of the best Turkish wines are produced. These unique wines, which include three types of white and three types of red wines, come from grapes grown organically since 1985. Oluş proudly presented the numerous awards that her wines have won, as well as future ventures, including the production of sparkling wine. As someone who comes from a country that has one of the largest number of state-owned vineyards in Southeastern Europe; where the tradition of growing vines and producing wine, especially red, is widespread; where we have many small producers, but also globally recognised wine producers, I was delighted with everything I saw at Vinolus. It was also interesting to see a woman at the helm of such a renowned wine brand, in an environment known for its traditional values. Of course, when you have the opportunity to hear a family story, and meet other successful women entrepreneurs from the Molu family, or stay in the beautiful Sunolus Vineyard House, you are not surprised. Each room in their small boutique hotel bears the name of a woman from the family and tells her life story through photos hung by the entrance door. This is another important and indispensable role of Sunolus Vineyard House. As a significant incentive for female entrepreneurship, it raises awareness and acknowledges the importance of business women.

Oluş, as our host, through this event provided an inspirational example of Gastrodiplomacy, representing family tradition and production, combined with Turkish hospitality. Oluş perhaps unconsciously presented the Republic of Türkiye in the best way, i.e. parts of the Turkish mentality, wealth of diversity, dynamicity and modernity.

*The visionaries behind the Gastrodiplomacy evening: (from left to right) JRE Board Member Gašper Puhan, Pristop Managing Director ernej Smisl, and Chef Gökhan Taşpınar.*

54

# Oluș Molu: Exploring the Journey of an Extraordinary Leader in Sustainable Farming and Holistic Living

Aysu İnsel, *Professor of Economics*

Oluș Molu and I have been friends for over forty years, ever since we were young girls. I believe it is only with the passing of several decades that we can fully appreciate the value of a very special, long-lasting friendship. We both know that the reality, quality, and existence of an eternal friendship is a treasure, deepened by mutually shared, experienced, and common memories over the years. Being Oluș's best friend, it is not easy for me to describe her unique characteristics and extraordinary achievements within a limited number of words. In the first instance, I see Oluș as a remarkable human being who could be best described by her exceptional qualities, her achievements, and our shared memories. Having said this, it is a privilege to share a few personal and heartfelt details about Molu Farm, the Molu family, and Oluș's remarkable attributes and accomplishments.

Having personally experienced the unique hospitality offered by the Molu family at Molu Farm over the years, I have always felt like a family member. I have witnessed their journey, from new beginnings to poignant endings. I have had the honour to be part of their lives, joining innovative meetings, and attending social and cultural events. And it's been a joy to witness the various modifications made by Oluș at the farm and consequent achievements during this time.

I believe that Oluș has the leadership skills to create new opportunities and to enhance both the natural environment and the diversity of agricultural production for farming. As a person, Oluș is enlightened, courageous, sophisticated, creative, and well-educated. She sincerely believes in two realities. Firstly, that ecological life as the highest form

> **Oluș believes that each and every day is a new day, and each day brings a new challenge as well as an opportunity to cherish; a new way to appreciate life to the full.**

of nature depends on applying knowledge, creativity, trust, and honesty; and secondly, developing a holistic outlook on life depends on love, kindness, sharing, reconciliation, and co-operation. Oluş has always enjoyed committing herself to researching, teaching, and sharing her knowledge; applying herself at various levels, whether that be one-to-one, locally, or globally. Through this, she has had a notable creative influence on both the community and the environment. In addition, I recognise that many people have been touched by her generosity, her genuineness, and have been influenced by her indomitable spirit and determination. She is always full of inspiration, always has an idea or the knowledge and motivation to create something new. Her creative spirit contributes not only to her own life, but to others around her, her farming life and the wider, natural environment. She accomplishes everything she sets her mind to do. Oluş believes that each and every day is a new day, and each day brings a new challenge as well as an opportunity to cherish; a new way to appreciate life to the full. There have been so many occasions where I have seen how Oluş applies multi-dimensionally thinking, finding solutions holistically. Over the years, I have also witnessed how she has fulfilled her dreams in spite of physical and emotional obstacles and risks. Oluş never gives up, she never loses hope or veers from the path she believes in.

It's well known that Oluş comes from a well-established, respected family in Kayseri. The Molu family are not only passionate about their family farm, but they have also been significant proponents of Kayseri for years. Respecting her family's legacy and cultural traditions, Oluş has led on important decisions and been behind a wide range of improvements at Molu Farm, whose story started back in the 1940s. Although Oluş appreciates and maintains much of the old farm, her innovative changes have helped to modernise and develop the property. Molu Farm is far from conventional, Oluş's unique approach to farming has led to the creation of an environmentally friendly, holistic property, with a focus on a sustainable relationship between humans and the natural environment. Despite traditional and environmental differences, challenges and risks, Oluş has consistently focused on a modern holistic farm model. And through this, she has made valuable contributions not only to the family farm, but also to the Turkish economy. And through it all, she has always had the moral support and financial backing from her late father Faruk Molu and her family.

Oluş's creative, innovative and original decisions have led to positive changes at the farm, helping to amplify the feasibility and diversity of its production. As part of these initiatives, Oluş achieved organic production certification at the farm, creating her artisanal wine brand and welcoming visitors to experience and taste her wines at her boutique hotel. Oluş first started producing Vinolus Wines in 2007. Soon after, she opened Sunolus Vineyard House in 2020 to encourage Eco-Tourism as well as Slow Tourism. Today, Oluş plays an important role in promoting wine culture and spreading the idea of Slow Tourism, specifically in the Cappadocia region and across Türkiye. Vinolus Vineyard House also offers wine tastings and sales alongside a variety of social events, creating awareness and promoting Türkiye's historical wine culture. From an academic perspective, Oluş has organised and led significant cultural and academic meetings, mainly in the field of gastronomy, to motivate and inspire academics, researchers, and students. Opening Sunolus Vineyard House has given her local, domestic and international guests the opportunity to enjoy the natural environment of the farm. Currently, Oluş is finalising her family project, "Meral and Metin Molu Foundation" which will serve as a Cultural and Education Centre promoting the unique holistic principles at Molu Farm.

*Let's have a little pri...*
*Oluş promoting Vino...*
*abro...*

Oluş has also instigated a number of pioneering achievements away from Molu Farm, from establishing the Cappadocia Organic Producers Union Association (KAPTAR) and popularising organic agriculture in Kayseri in 2009; to launching a start-up project on organic agriculture with 50 producers in 2011 with the support of Kayseri Provincial Directorate of Agriculture. In 2013, Oluş initiated the opening of the first seasonal organic, (fresh vegetables and fruit) market in Kayseri via an agreement with the local municipalities and a protocol with the Wheat Ecological Life Support Association. This was followed by consulting on Türkiye's first Hobby Garden for Kayseri Metropolitan Municipality in 2017; and supporting the Women's Cooperative within KAPTAR in 2018 by championing the collective work of organic agricultural production.

My words can only briefly reflect Oluş's wide ranging achievements, her caring personality and on-going commitments. What is clear is that she is not only a creative and innovative person but also a good person, and an authentic, forward-thinking leader for women in Türkiye. I deeply believe that her big heart is focused on giving, her bright mind is constantly creating, her unique friendships are based on integrity, and her well-intentioned life is all about helping all those that reside on our blue planet.

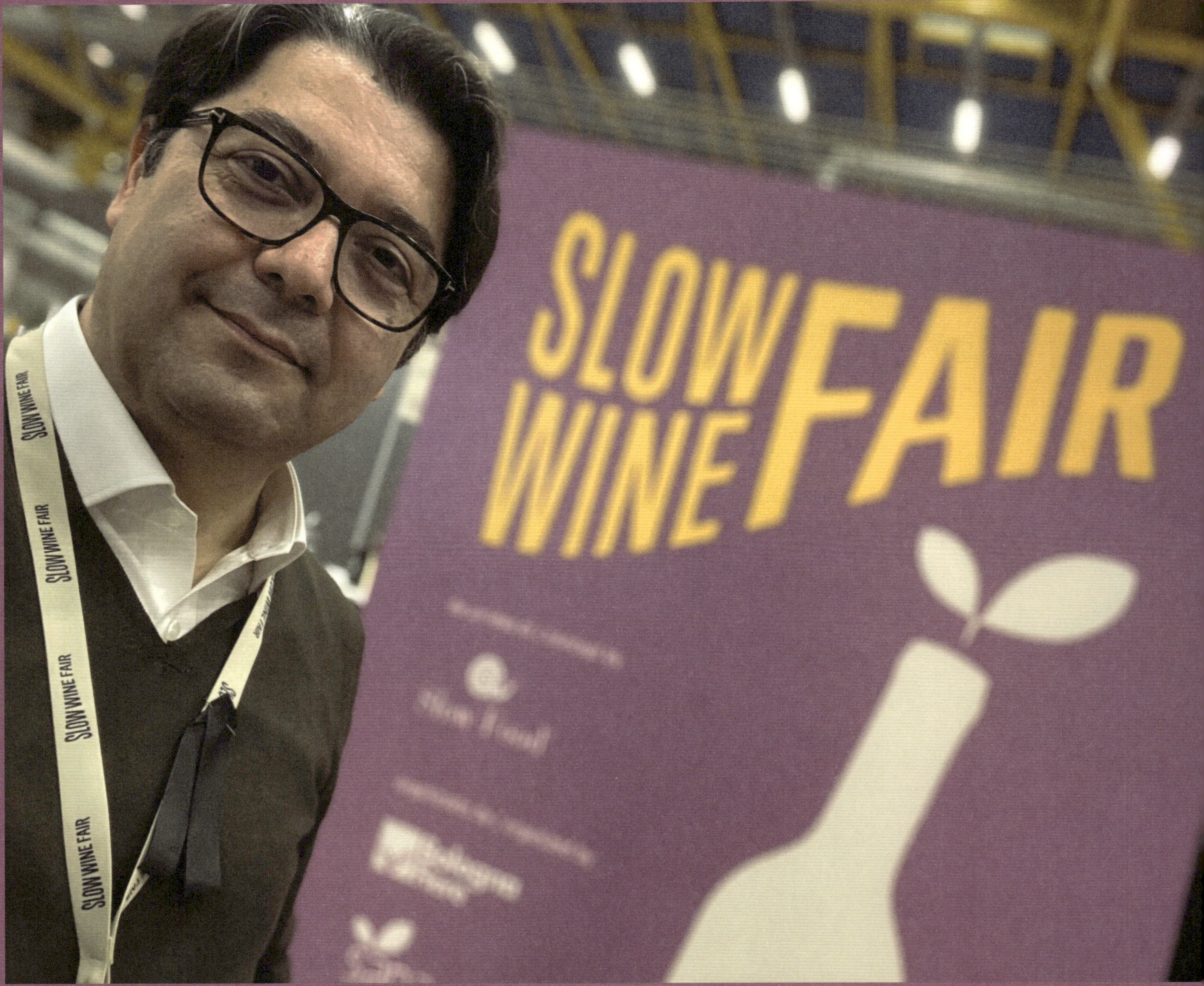
SLOW WINE FAIR
SLOW WINE FAIR

# Perception of Champagne Among The Ottoman Elite

**Dr. İnanç Atılgan,** *Cultural Scientist, JRE Representative to Türkiye*

My contribution explores the hypocrisy of the Ottoman elite towards champagne and wine, with a focus on how they navigated around the cultural and religious norms surrounding alcohol. Despite the Islamic prohibition of alcohol, historical sources reveal that champagne, among other alcoholic drinks, was consumed and even celebrated by some Ottoman elites. This article delves into the historical context, cultural influences, and attitudes towards wine and champagne among the Ottomans.

It was from the Arabs of Andalusia (711 AD to 1492 AD) that we adopted the Arabic word "Al-kuhûl" or "Alcohol". During that time, physicians, especially in Europe believed that this foreign alcohol could be a medicine capable of overcoming illnesses. This alcoholic beverage, which helped people to ease their pains and feel more comfortable, was referred to as "aqua vitae" (Water of Life) in Europe. The Greek phrase "hydôr bios," meaning "water of life," evolved into Latin as "aqua vitae." The original term for the Turkish word "ispirto" (Italian: "spirito"), which came from the West, is also derived from the Latin "spiritus" (essence of life, soul, spirit). Isn't it true that when we consume alcohol in a cultured and moderate manner, it brings about both a sense of happiness and subtle medicinal qualities?

> **When it suits, champagne is alcohol; when it doesn't suit, it's medicine.**

### Wine in Pre-Islamic and Islamic Turkish Culture

Wine was of significant importance in the pre-Islamic (up to the end of the 10th century) and Islamic periods of Turkish history. It is generally accepted that the old Turkish word for wine is "süçig", which means "sweet, wine", a word used during these times. Alcohol, as in many other cultures around the world, plays an important role in contemporary Turkish society. As I mentioned, the Turks used to call wine "süci" or "bor," "çağır," amongst other similar names. Specifically, among Western Turks, due to the influence of Islam, these ancient words have generally been replaced by the Arabic term "şarap" for wine.

In certain Turkish communities, there is still a tradition of creating "kımız," a national beverage made from horse's milk using a special fermentation method in containers known as "saba". Particularly today, "kımız" is still considered a remedy for some illnesses in Bashkortostan. Additionally, Turks have produced a drink similar to the aperitif, rakı known as "ayran arağası" by allowing ayran (a salted yoghurt drink) to remain in amphorae and oak vessels for an extended period of time. The Central Asian Turks were also aware of the Chinese "rice wine." As our topic relates to grapes, we will move on to focus on wine.

According to Tietze, in Old Ottoman Turkish, the word "ayak" also means "cup for drinking alcohol" or "chalice," (in addition to its regular meaning of "foot"). Depictions of rulers and individuals holding cups attributed to the Göktürks and Uighurs show that the Turks also placed great importance on drinking vessels like "çağırlığ ayak" (wine glass) and "altun ayak," "kengeş ayak" (assembly cup). Additionally, the Turks also used the words "sağrak" and "idiş" to refer to a drinking cup.

**Wine Culture in The Ottoman Empire**

There have always been prejudices regarding the consumption of alcoholic beverages in predominantly Muslim countries. It has been made evident that, contrary to the prohibition in the Quran, many Turks consumed champagne, sherry, or rakı under the label of "medicine". Zugmayer writes in 1899: *"Even the Temperance movement followers allow these types as "medicinal wines" to pass through, similar to how the Turks treat champagne."*

## Despite the strict prohibitions of Islam, consumption of alcohol was common throughout the Ottoman Empire's history.

*The Turk in a tavern in Istanbul Miniature by Fazıl Enderun (Hubanname Zenanname, 1793, Istanbul University Library*

Accounts of travellers visiting the Ottoman Empire provide ample evidence. The Austrian Ambassador to the Ottoman Empire, Ogier Ghislain de Busbecq, who during his time in Constantinople around 1550, recounts at the beginning of his journey how the sweet

Young Turks welcoming cultural modernisation and Westernisation, wine experienced a renaissance across Turkish society, with several Austrian newsletters from the 19th century accounting for the high level of wine appreciation across the Ottoman Empire.

Despite the strict prohibitions of Islam, consumption of alcohol was common throughout the Ottoman Empire's history. In particular, champagne and other alcoholic beverages were consumed by the Ottoman elites both for medical purposes and as a status symbol.

Champagne, in particular, was viewed not just as "wine" but as a "medicinal drink" or "sherbet," thus circumventing religious prohibitions.

Historical sources indicate that significant figures, including Ottoman sultans, consumed champagne and other alcoholic beverages. Cornelius Gurlitt's 1912 article provides insights into alcohol consumption of the Ottoman Turks. Gurlitt details how wine and other alcoholic beverages were consumed despite the prohibitions, whilst Mehmed Tevfik's works like "Treatise on Alcohol and Gambling" [İçki ve Kumar Risalesi] in the late 19th and early 20th century explore, in a critical yet humorous way, the taverns and drinking habits in Istanbul, emphasising the widespread alcohol consumption and its impact on social life. Despite the prohibition, enforcing it proved challenging. Gurlitt notes that alcohol consumption was not just a social activity but also used for medical purposes, amongst other European observers who documented alcohol consumption in Ottoman society: "*In the Ottoman Empire, it was champagne that held a superior standing compared to other alcoholic beverages. As a symbol of status and prestige, Ottoman elites sipped on champagne during social gatherings, official ceremonies, and private occasions, bypassing religious bans.*"

Hungarian wine "tempted" the Turks: "*The less they have of it, the more eager they are for it. They press the envoy's staff to give them wine, which exposes them to serious dangers. Throughout the ages, one encounters the same difficulty: distinguished and common Turks demand more or less brazenly that Christians give them wine, drink themselves "wild and full" at the table, and pay no heed to the inconveniences they cause their hosts before the Turkish authorities. The envoys themselves are often embarrassed when even the leading statesmen of the Porte daily send their servants to them for wine.*"

Despite the Quran's prohibition of wine consumption, the Ottoman Empire was renowned for growing high-quality grape varieties. The Quran banned the consumption of wine but did not prohibit viticulture. Even though the consumption of wine was prohibited, wines from other countries were imported into the Ottoman Empire. With the reign of the

*Historical sources reveal that Ottoman sultans, including Sultan Bayezid I and Bayezid II, were known for their appreciation of wine. Despite the prohibitions, champagne and other alcoholic beverages found their way into Ottoman society, providing a nuanced understanding of the attitudes towards alcohol among the Ottoman elites.*

*The perception of champagne among the Ottoman elite as a medicinal drink allowed them to bypass religious bans on wine consumption. The Grazer Zeitung reports the following on May 12, 1838 on page 15: "In Constantinople, the Sultan has ordered the building of a beet sugar factory. A champagne factory (which the Turks sell as sorbet*

61

*rather than wine) is also to be set up there."* A Viennese reporter, F. L. Hübsch, acts here as an interesting information source of Turkish merchants and how they behaved abroad, in relation to wine consumption: *"It is not uncommon for one to hear the strange sounding words in the wine houses of Vienna: "Scherabi getir" (i.e. bring wine) ring out, and if one looks around for the place from which they came, one sees a Turk, who later enjoys abottle of 1834 Grinzinger or Meidlinger [wine] without thinking about the prohibition in the Quran; yes, since champagne wine is no longer wine according to modern Turkish concepts, the rich merchants from Constantinople, who stay in our imperial city [Vienna] for a long time because of their trade, leave on happy occasions, especially when their business has taken a happy turn in honour of the prophet's beard some cork rise against the morning side, popping, as a sign that thee njoyment of joy is not announced by shooting bollards like their self-conscious ancestors once did, but by the harmless, fragrant gas that escapes from a champagne bottle. The late Sultan seems to have removed the bandage ofprejudice from the Muslims; But not only in Constantinople, but even in the smaller towns of the Turkish Empire, the necks of various bottles are diligently guillotined and their golden liquid contents are jubilantly sacrificed to Allah and his chosen prophet. The Mohammedan casuists not only seem to like this innovation, but rather to favour it; because they are now trying to prove clearly and clearly even from the Quran that for example, cider is one of the drinks that the sons of Mohammed may allow to entertheir inner beings without hesitation and without any loss of happiness. Should a devout Muslim make sharp remarks about it, the champagne Turks usually excuse themselves by saying that it is pure apple cider; and thus, such a white lie gave him no cause for trouble. According to a trade report from Odessa baskets of champagne wine are said to have left France for Constantinople in 1843; of which 405 baskets were addressed to Turkish and Armenian merchants, the rest to German and French merchant houses."* (Hübsch 104)

"The Komischen Briefe" of Hans-Jörgel of Gumpoldskirchen near Vienna was a humorous Austrian monthly magazine that was published in Vienna between 1832 and 1851. It was released by the publisher of the Imperial and Royal Court and State Printing Office. In Jörgel Letters of 6th of June 1863 p. 5, we read: *"Viennese Beer and Styrian Champagne in Istanbul: The Styrian Champagne (Crème de Styrie*

*from Kleinoscheg in Graz) is, in fact, more durable and costs half as much as French Champagne, achieving the same delightful taste. The Turks are beginning to appreciate the taste of this product made from Styrian grapes, and an acquaintance who offered a few glasses to a Turk experienced the following amusing scene. Just as the affable Turk had finished his third glass, another person rushed up to him and exclaimed, "Ali! For Allah's sake, you're not drinking wine, are you?" "Be quiet, Hassan," said Ali, "it's Styrian Champagne from Kleinoscheg. I've known about it since my first trip to Vienna. The Prophet will forgive me for the sin." With that, Ali finished his glass. When Hassan saw this, he asked Ali for a glass as well. Eventually, both Ali and Hassan were in high spirits, and Ali poured another glass for Hassan. In the end, both Ali and Hassan were cheerful. As for me, I had the three of them sketched as in-laws: the Viennese, Ali, and Hassan."*

The consumption of champagne and other alcoholic beverages in the Ottoman Empire, despite the prohibitions of Islam, held significant importance. Historical sources demonstrate that Ottoman elites consumed champagne both for medical purposes and as a status symbol. This article contributes to the understanding of alcohol culture in the Ottoman Empire by examining the consumption of champagne in a historical and cultural context.

I would like to conclude my contribution with a quote from Marianna Yerasimos, a well-known author and food historian of Greek descent from Istanbul. She has authored several books and articles that explore the rich history and diversity of Turkish food culture, often focusing on the connections between food, history, and cultural identity: *"While a significant portion of Ottoman society certainly refrained from consuming wine, which was considered forbidden, it was also Muslim Ottomans who wrote countless poems praising wine, composed 'sakiname' [book of the cupbearer] poems about drinking gatherings, and produced volumes of 'ays u isret' [pleasure and revelry] and 'ays u tarab' [pleasure and joy] literature. The infamous drinkers of Istanbul who have gone down in history were also Muslim Ottomans. Those who frequented the 1,060 taverns in Istanbul and turned alcohol sales into a profitable profession were certainly not just the 'infidels' embodying every sinful habit."* (Yerasimos, 216)

Finally, to sum up: When it suits, champagne is alcohol; when it doesn't suit, it's medicine.

**References**

Andreas Tietze, "Tarihî ve Etimolojik Türkiye Türkçesi Lugati" [Historical and Etymological Dictionary of Turkish Language of Türkiye], TÜBA, 2022.

Caşteğin Turgunbayer and İsi Hasan, "Kısrak Sütünden Şaraba Eski Türk Kültüründe Süçig Kelimesi Üzerine Değerlendirmeler" [Evaluations on the Word 'Süçig' in Ancient Turkish Culture: From Mare's Milk to Wine], Türkbilig, 2021.

Cornelius Gurlitt, "Der Alkoholismus bei den Türken" [Alcoholism Among the Turks], Neue Freie Presse, January 15, 1912.

F. L. Hübsch, "Die Worte des Propheten verhallen" [The Words of the Prophet Fade Away], Ost und West Blätter für Kunst Literatur und geselliges Leben, April 1, 1845.

Jelena Mrgic, "Aqua vitae – Notes on Geographies of Alcohol Production and Consumption in the Ottoman Balkans", Issues in Ethnology and Anthropology, 2017.

Marianna Yerasimos, Evliya Çelebi Seyahatnamesi'nde Yemek Kültürü [Culinary Culture in Evliya Çelebi's Book of Travels]. İstanbul 2011.

Peter Zieme, "Alkoholische Getränke bei den alten Türken" [Alcoholic Beverages Among the Ancient Turks], SZTE OJS Journals, 2022.

Zugmayer, Erich, "Reisebilder aus Skandinavien" [Travel Images from Scandinavia]. Radfahr-Sport, 1.12.1899, Nr. 48, P. 827.

PS: I am proud to have had the honor of introducing the first Turkish wine in Vienna on January 20, 2005, with Kavaklıdere Wines' "Selection Red" and "Narince.

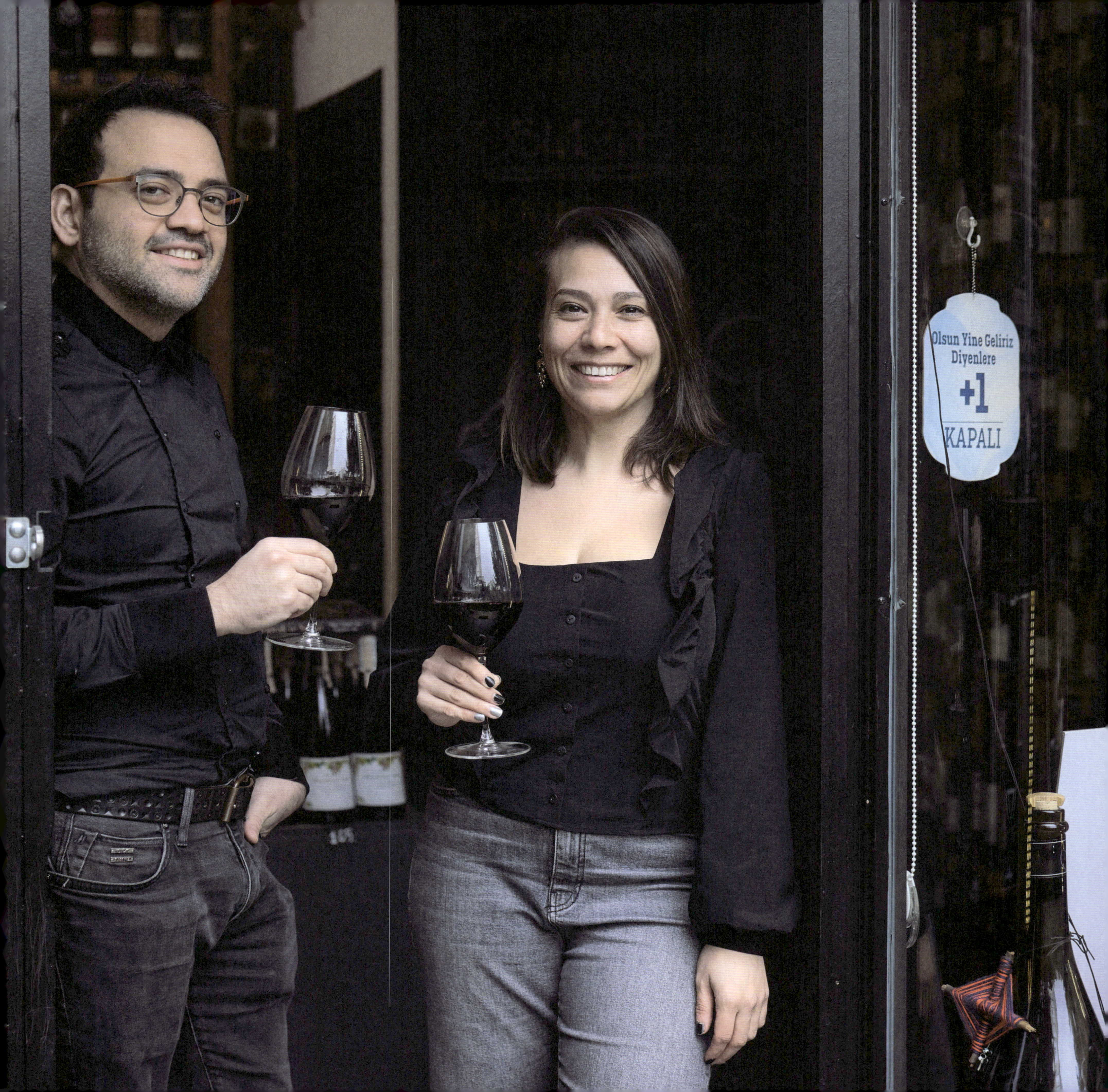
Olsun Yine Geliriz
Diyenlere
+1
KAPALI

# From Vine to Wine: The Journey of Vinolus in Anatolia

**Süray Cingöz Atış & Doğuhan Atış,**
*Wine Experts, Owners of Santé Wine & More*

Oluş Molu, the founder of Vinolus, graduated from the Biology Department of Hacettepe University. After graduation, she continued her academic career holding various positions in public institutions. In her own words, she was "still searching" when she received her father's call to "return home" and found herself starting a new chapter in Kayseri in 2007.

A significant part of Oluş's childhood was spent on the 2.000 acre Arif Molu Farm, named after her grandfather. Here, her love for nature developed through her fascination for the natural environment, and inspired her future endeavours, including organic farming. Oluş was the first to receive an organic farming certificate in Kayseri and has been striving to promote this sustainable method of production in the region ever since.

> Her love for nature developed through her fascination for the natural environment and inspired her future endeavours, including organic farming.

The second part of this story begins with Oluş's encounter with wine grapes in the vineyard. Although the farm primarily grew table grapes, at one time, her father Faruk Molu, at the insistence of a friend, grafted some of his vines with wine-growing varieties, Chardonnay and Kalecik Karası. As a wine lover who enjoyed wine at her table, Oluş decided to focus on viticulture, knowing how valuable wine was as a product. Expanding the existing vineyard area to 120 acres, by 2009 Oluş had added Narince, Roussanne, and Tempranillo to her portfolio of grape varietals grown, alongside the Chardonnay and Kalecik Karası.

The vineyard, located at an altitude of 1,050 metres, is certified organic, planted and managed using organic farming methods, fighting pests

*Atış, Süray Cingöz & Doğuhan: Toprak ve Şarap [Soil and Wine: Vineyards and Wines of Türkiye]. 2022 Istanbul (ISBN 978-625-7491-84-6).*

naturally without the use of chemicals. The volcanic soils, containing sand and clay, are rich in minerals yet poor in organic matter, providing the vines with all they need. The continental climate conditions, along with low humidity and seasonal winds help to create wide diurnal temperature differences between day and night, allowing the grapes to preserve their aromas and ripen slowly.

Today, Molu Farm is home to both conventional and organic farming, a forest of pine and cedar trees, a range of livestock providing meat and milk, and the Vinolus winery, with a production of approximately thirty-five thousand bottles annually. In addition to wine, local items such as molasses, tomato paste, jam, noodles, flour, bulgur, wheat, tarhana, walnut sausage, and köfter (molasses delight) are also made here.

The most recent development at the farm is the Sunolus Guest House, which opened in 2020 with eight guestrooms. Visitors are invited to sample local Kayseri dishes at the restaurant at the vineyard house, or enjoy a tranquil tasting of Vinolus wines.

### Vinolus Wines

Prioritising quality over quantity, the low-volume production at the vineyard means Oluş has time to pay close attention to each of her wines, with a focus on their flavour profiles. Her white wines are particularly noteworthy. The Chardonnay, aged in oak barrels and left on its lees, stands out with its smoky notes balanced by white-fleshed fruit tones like apple, pear, and quince; supported by a creamy texture on the palate alongside lively acidity and mineral notes. The only downside is that this wine is produced in such limited quantities!

Vinolus typically produces two different wines made from Narince. The first uses grapes from Tokat, the homeland of the grape variety, while the second is made from grapes from the farm's vineyards, produced organically. These two examples stand out as white wines with character, liveliness, and a satisfying palate. The consistent use of moderate oak ageing year after year is commendable.

Our producer's one white blend reflects Oluş's quest for uniqueness, and the result is an interesting wine combining Emir, known for its striking acidity and minerality and sourced externally, with Roussanne, a French grape from her own vineyards, noted for its fresh, aromatic structure.

In some vintages, Vinolus produces a dark pink wine by blending Kalecik Karası with Syrah, and sometimes Tempranillo. There is also a red wine released under the name "Blend," made by combining Kalecik Karası and Syrah. Oluş's other red wines are created as single-varietal wines, Kalecik Karası and Syrah.

Vinolus Kalecik Karası, dominated by cotton candy aromas, is one of the most original interpretations of the grape. With little to no oak influence, its red colour, soft tannins, the quality of the fruit, and lively acidity that tickles the palate make it stand out, whilst its body and structure differentiate it from other wines made with Kalecik Karası.

Looking at Vinolus Syrah, we see that the grapes are sourced from the high plateau Güney district of Denizli. Syrah as a variety performs very well in the Güney district, successfully creating a distinct style of Syrah. The Vinolus Syrah is a perfect example, it is not a muscular, heavy Syrah; rather, it attracts attention with its elegance. While the oak influence stays in the background, the fruitiness of this red wine comes to the forefront, supported by velvety tannins.

PS: This article was translated into English from the authors' 2022 book "Toprak ve Şarap: Türkiye'nin Bağları ve Şarapları" [Soil and Wine: Vineyards and Wines of Türkiye], with their permission and without any additions (ISBN 978-625-7491-84-6, pages 328-330).

> With a focus on quality over quantity, the low-volume production at the vineyard means Oluş has time to pay close attention to each of her wines.

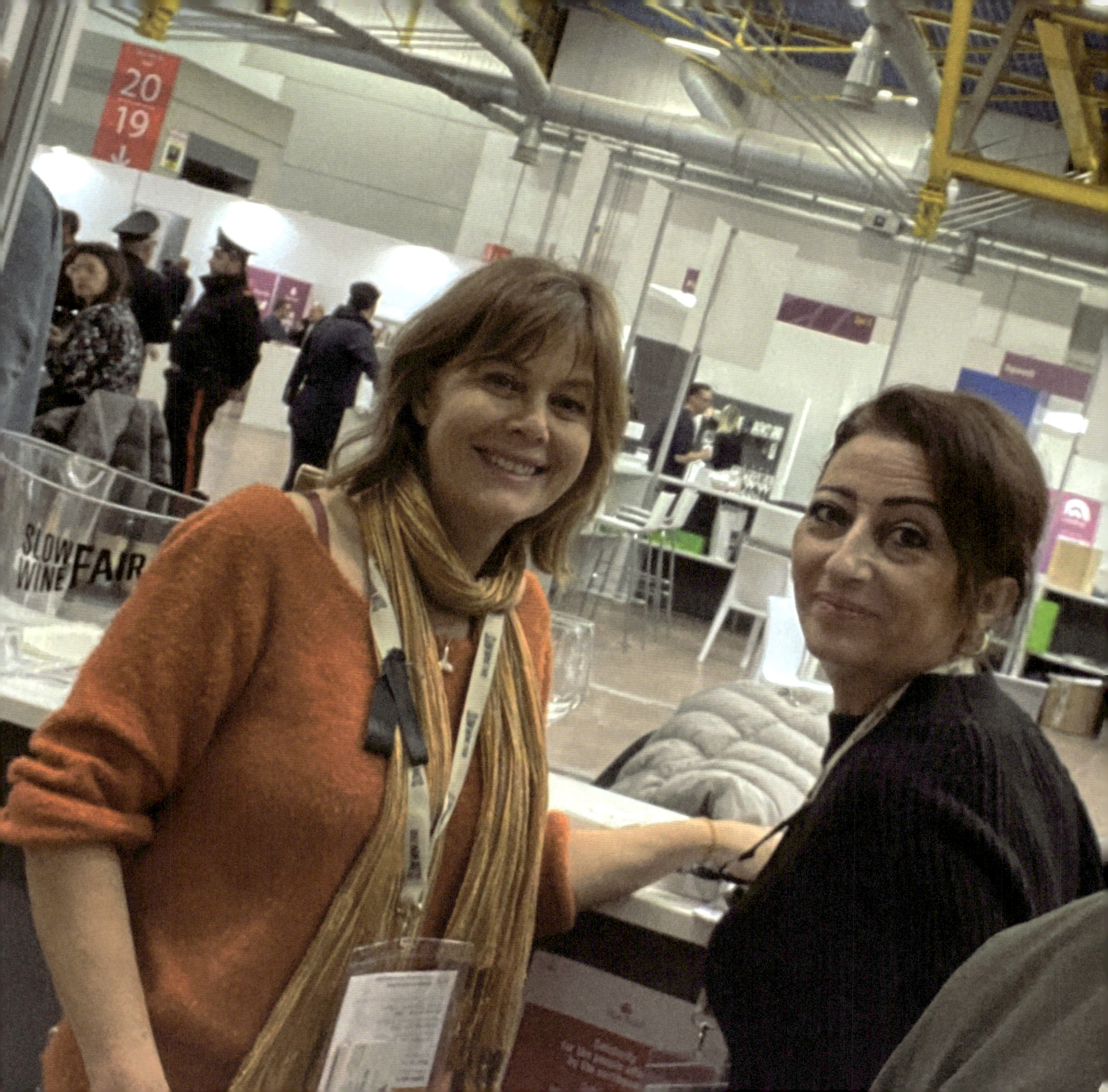
20
19
SLOW
WINE FAIR

# Multicultural Background of Oluş and Its Impact on Vinolus

Pınar Akkaya *DipWSET*

Around eight thousand years ago, history tell us that wine enthusiasts in Mesopotamia regularly, and patiently waited for their grapes to ferment and turn into their favourite drink, a drink to mark a celebration, a special occasion, or a simple dinner after a busy day.

When we mention wine, we are talking about a drink that is as old as human civilisation. Indeed, there are only a few things as old as wine that have travelled alongside humans throughout history. From the fermentation of the very first bunch of grapes, wine has remained at the heart of social life in most civilisations; wine has been at the centre of life's celebrations and rites of passage, perceived both as a religious and prestigious status symbol. Wine has been the choice of drink of kings and the elite, not only during their earthly lives but also after they have departed this world. The notorious Egyptian pharaoh Tutankhamun is said to have been buried with 5,000 post-mortem gifts which included around 26 carefully selected bottles that he could enjoy in the afterlife, tagged with the name of the winemaker and the name of the varietal; each harvested in 1345, 1344 or 1340 BC, obviously the best vintages of his lifetime.

> Wine helps to fuel creativity like culture; it nurtures ideas and reveals the true personality of a person.

Wine also reflects the social hierarchy of its time. Though wine producers and consumers have historically been high ranking clergy men and kings, ordinary people also enjoyed what was considered a prestigious beverage, as much as they were allowed to and whenever they had the opportunity to do so. Around 515 BC, in Persepolis, an ancient city close to modern day Shiraz in Iran, every citizen was endowed with a certain amount of wine depending on their social status, gender, profession, or age. Wherever vines are planted around the world, harvests have always offered an opportunity to celebrate a new stage of the year, and an association with prosperity and joy of life.

Even though it was the Greeks who spread their culture of wine across the Mediterranean, introducing Vitis Vinifera, some may argue that it was the Romans who were the architects of today's wine panorama. The moment you begin to explore a particular European country's history about wine, it is almost impossible not to feel the impact and presence of the Romans. As wine was an essential part of their life, they were renowned for importing and planting vines wherever they reigned during their long history. Romans not only produced and consumed wine but also traded it successfully, creating a legacy that paved the way to the wine industry we know today.

*"May you be immortal, these wines are all good and fine, the wine of Transoxania, when they prepare it well, the wine of Herat, the wine of Marw-Rud, the wine of Bust and the must of Hulwan, but no wine can ever compare with the Babylonian wine and the must of Bazrang."* Script found on a document of the Sassanian Empire period, 224-651 AD.

Today, wine is still accepted as a cultural symbol and attracts interest across the globe and by people from all walks of life, as an essential part of gastronomic culture and social relations. Though its link to religion has weakened somewhat over time, its presence in milestone celebrations and special occasions is stronger than ever. It is also a major economic source of income for key wine producing countries. With the effects of climate change and average temperatures shifting across the globe, new players are starting to emerge on the scene, making the wine world even more dynamic and interesting for consumers and wine connoisseurs alike. With its long history and strong social standing, wine offers a rich culture that embraces everyone who appreciates it.

## Where wine and culture meet

I must say that I am fortunate to oscillate between two wonderful worlds: The world of wine and the world of culture. On the one hand, I work in a cross cultural domain, speaking at and facilitating training programmes on national and business cultures. On the other hand, I work in wine, as a consultant and educator. My two seemingly unrelated worlds have a lot more in common than you'd initially expect. First, wine is closely related to culture and second, it is as complex as culture. This is probably why the conversation always comes back to culture whenever I mention that I work in wine.

Before I make this connection a little clearer, let me share some fundamental information on culture in the way we use it in the cross cultural domain. Culture is defined by Hosftede, one of the pioneers of cultural studies, as "the software of the mind". Culture is the lifeblood of a society. Culture is why we behave in a certain way, how we celebrate things, how we have fun, the way we perceive the past and the future, and the way we build interpersonal relationships. As expressed in this beautiful anonymous definition, "culture is the water we swim in".

Culture is multilayered, like an onion, if I use an analogy used by many culturalists. There is the national culture, which peeled back reveals the regional culture, followed by the minority group culture, company culture, team culture and finally individual culture. Even thinking about these layers may help you understand how complex culture can be. However in the end, the culture we are born into affects our perspective, our values, and our behaviour towards others. Using the water analogy above, very often we do not know how the water we swim in tastes unless we spend some time outside it.

Culture is also bound to stereotypes, or the somewhat spontaneous ideas or perceptions about people, usually made only because they come from a certain culture, for example thinking that Italians will always like pizza and that they are unable to speak without using their hands - which obviously is not the case.

As I have mentioned earlier, the most important commonality between wine and culture is the fact that both are very complex. Understanding wine is as complex as understanding culture. The more one learns about the wine, the more one understands they will never know everything about it. Same goes for culture, the more you go into the detail of different cultures, the more you see how complex it is.

One particular point where wine and culture meet is possibly our palates. Biologically speaking, culture can indeed make an impact on our perception of aromas and flavours due to different sensitivity levels of our palates. Going further, the origin of a wine, its price, the occasion in which we enjoy it, or the environment we consume it may also have a cultural influence on our perception. I came across some interesting research while I was looking into the link between wine and culture. In 2019, two social scientists, Rodrigues and Parr, explored how culture influenced wine preferences in drinkers. Their research examined the influence of culture based on our sensory attributes to wine, external factors such as the label, the price or factual information about the wine, our conceptual understanding such as production methods and our emotional responses to wine, mainly how the wine we drink make us feel. Rodrigues and Parr concluded their research by stating that there were no consistent findings to support the role of wine familiarity or availability on our preferences for wines. However, several studies in their research showed the importance of our previous experiences on how we understand and appreciate wine, which means we are coming back to the place where culture and wine meet.

### The ancient world

In the wine community, professionals have the habit of referring to wine producing countries of continental Europe as the "Old World" and the rest of the world as the "New World". This has started to change as the industry is now using "Europe" and "Outside Europe" to refer to these countries and their wines.

This being the case, I have always felt that Türkiye was not correctly referred to as a wine producing country: It is certainly not a New World country, but Old World does not seem to be the right fit for Türkiye, either, considering its link to the origins of wine. Then, during my visit to Burgundy this summer, I bought an interesting wine book, "La Carte des Vins, s'il vous plait" published by Marabout Publications in 2018, that focused on wine maps, exploring wine through a geographical lens. As I read through the first few pages of the book, I turned the page and was surprised to see a map that included Türkiye, Georgia and Armenia with a note on the side that said: "This is where our journey starts. Not very surprising that the wine saw the daylight in the region that your geography teacher referred as "The Fertile Croissant" at school."

> **There is untapped potential in Cappadocia; the local varieties and the terroir are yet to be fully studied.**

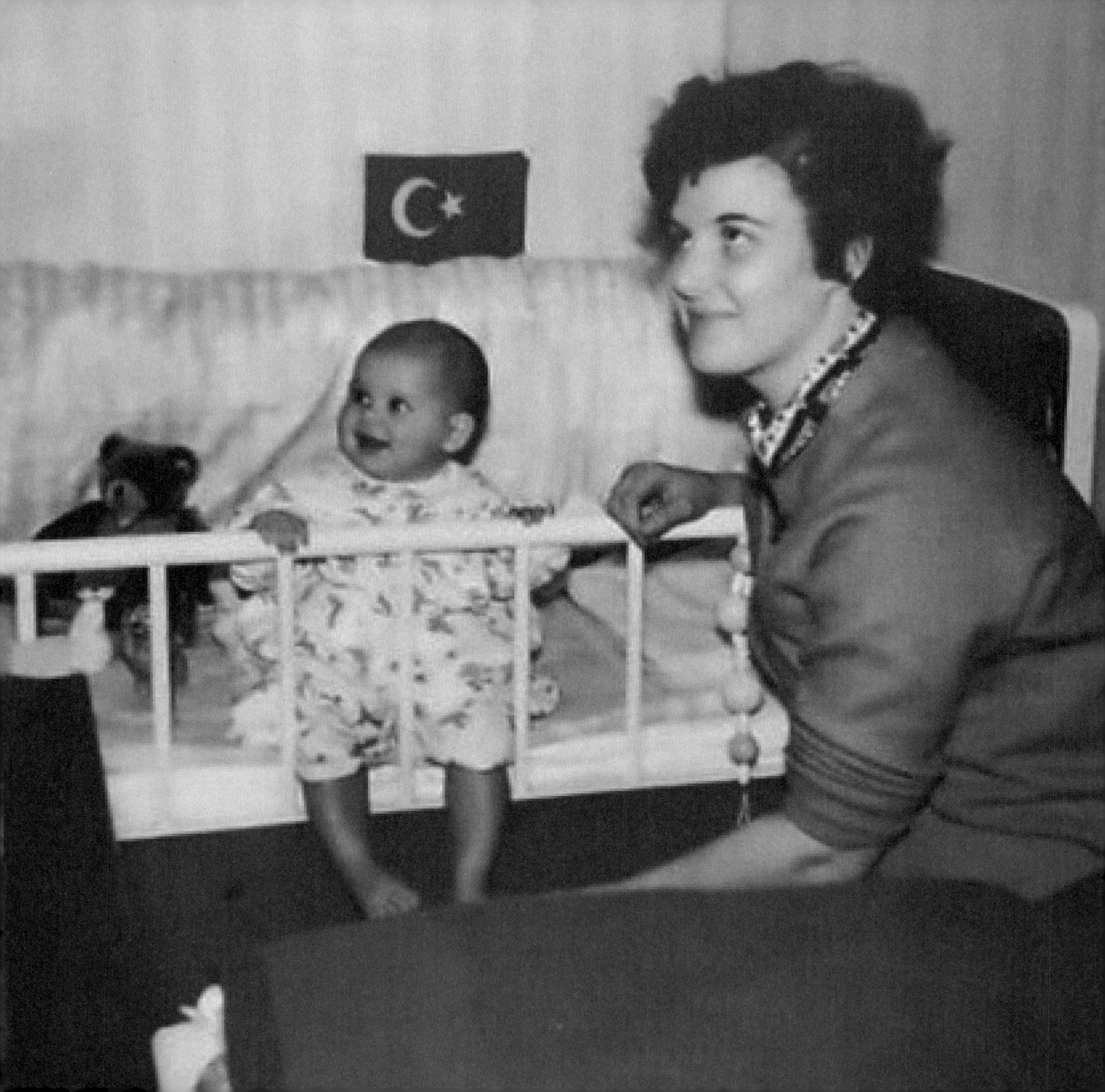

It is true that together with today's Georgia and Armenia, Türkiye fits into the "Ancient World" description, due to its history of thousands of years as a wine producer. The first written records of wine and wine culture in Mesopotamia and Anatolia have been found in archaeological digs and these records mention winemaking and wine consumption across the region, highlighting the role of wine in society as a symbol of wealth, prosperity, and fertility. Wine was not only produced locally but also imported from one of its neighbours, modern day Armenia. There are records in cuneiform texts that indicate some of the wine was also imported from Iran via traders.

### Cappadocia: A multicultural land

Among all these places in the 'fertile croissant' and neighbouring Anatolia, Cappadoccia has a very special place. Positioned in the north of the Taurus mountains, this beautiful region is unique, its geographical structures featuring fairytale scenes of little towers of soft volcanic rock, mysterious caves and a patchwork of colours that change their palette from dawn to dusk. Cappadocia is also home to a number of rare indigenous grapes such as Kalecik Karasi and Emir, producing excellent wines thanks to its volcanic soil and ideal climate for grape growing. With a long tradition of winemaking that can be traced back to Hittites, Cappadocia is another place where wine and culture meet.

*Iluş in her room in Kiel, Germany with her mother.*

*Sıla Serim is following in the footsteps of her mother, Oluş. She completed her Master's in Luxury Brand Management in London. A worthy member of the Molu family.*

## Oluş Molu: An exceptional woman producing wine in the heart of Anatolia

Being a woman working in wine is difficult wherever you are in the world. The wine industry is a notoriously male dominated arena where a handful of women attempt to create awareness and navigate against the wave. This is changing however, women are transforming the industry one step at a time, as winemakers, wine producers and grape growers. More women are stepping up and making their voices heard as educators, wine experts, wine writers and more. These are strong women who know where they want to go and what they want to do. Fathers are now leaving their legacy to their daughters. Oluş being one of them.

Unlike the big cities like Istanbul or Izmir, Kayseri - where Oluş produces her wines - remains a relatively conservative city. Being a woman wine producer in Kayseri is not easy, it requires flexibility, ambition, clarity, and a drive for success. Oluş did not see these as obstacles to stop her from what she wanted to do. "I know this is not something that many people would imagine achieving under these circumstances. But it was enough for me to have the physical conditions to produce wine and I have had these. I stick to my own values, and these give me the power I need."

Growing up, Oluş was nurtured by the richness of different cultures in her family, clearly motivated and inspired by the unique, modern perspectives of her parents. Her father was an open-minded Turkish man who studied abroad; whilst her mother, who was born and raised in Germany, spent much of her life in Türkiye, following the man she fell in love with. It was these two individuals, who having a great love for each other made every effort to give their children the best of both cultures and to support them in whatever they wished to do. There were certainly moments of tension as well due to differences in perspectives, or differences in values, especially in Oluş's childhood and adolescence. This is something that I often hear from people growing up in mixed families, which also explains the complexity of different cultural backgrounds when it comes to bringing up children. Especially when there may be differences between parents in their belief systems and etiquette which may create contradictions in how they lead their lives.

One major difference related to relationships between women and men. While the German culture saw the proximity between a man and a woman as a sign of love and trust, the Turkish culture had restrictions on that matter and the proximity was perceived as a problem since it was a threat to a person's chastity.

Another difference was language. Multicultural childhoods often leads to multilingual children, it is the children in the family that learn languages quickly even if it is not spoken at home, meaning the languages of the parents are usually acquired quickly. However, in Oluş's case, speaking German was not encouraged at home and she would only speak it with her mother. The fact of not being able to express herself in one of her native languages made her reflect more and learn about herself as a young person. Oluş told me that these reflections helped her know herself better and express her feelings and ideas in a more effective way later in life. These differences also made young Oluş think about and question things at an early age. She ended up finding her own way and building her own approach to many things. Oluş believes that one cannot protect a culture by imposing a fear of losing certain values or beliefs, because she thinks this causes the culture to lose its richness and depth.

Culture is very closely linked to values. When you grow in a multicultural environment, you end up building your own set of values nurtured by every culture you interacted with. For everyone, there are some values that are non-negotiable, the ones that we are not willing to adapt, nor change depending on the situation. Ever since we met a few years ago, my talks with Oluş usually revolve around life, our reactions to life's events and about our values that make us react in a certain way. What I find in her is a true sense of humanism. In my opinion, what Oluş describes as her values is very much aligned with "being a mensch", a term I first read in Guy Kawasaki's book, "The Art of The Start." A mensch is a person of integrity, morality, dignity, with a sense of what is right and responsible. Oluş's compass always orientates her towards being a mensch and acting as one no matter what her personal interest is.

## Swimming in several waters

Having grown up in a mixed family with a German mother and Turkish father, in a city considered to be the cradle of Anatolian civilisations, producing wine where the early Christians created their first villages and as a woman entrepreneur, for me, Oluş embodies a multicultural background.

During one of our conversations, I asked Oluş what being multicultural meant to her. I was curious to hear her own definition as a person who comes from a multicultural background. However, her definition is not a usual one, Oluş does not see multiculturalism as a phenomenon that forms a homogenous structure by combining different cultures under a single umbrella. Instead, she adopts a more holistic perspective and thinks that multiculturalism cannot be defined statically since culture itself is a dynamic and ever-changing phenomenon. Departing from this dynamic point of view, Oluş thinks that multiculturalism also nurtures creativity with its ever-changing nature, linking back to a great potential for creativity. It sounds like creativity is one of her own driving forces as well, seeing what she has done so far in winemaking for Vinolus and hospitality with Sunolus. For example, just like her mother used to do when she was a child, Oluş often combines Turkish and German cuisines to create new dishes and offer these in her hotel's restaurant.

In hospitality, cultural awareness and cultural dexterity are critical skills. Oluş's natural acquisition of these skills since the early years of her life made it easier for her to build bridges between people arriving from different parts of the world, each with different expectations and anticipations when it comes to their holiday, food, drink and travelling.

With my mind wandering in this lovely garden of wine and culture, I also wanted to see what Oluş thought about wine from a cultural perspective, especially as a woman who produces wine in not only one of the oldest wine regions but also the cradle of ancient civilisations. Wine is no doubt a social drink. It creates links between people, facilitates conversations, and it is a great topic of discussion for those who are particularly interested in wine. Historically, key gatherings, dinners and meetings were always organised alongside good wine. It looks like we have a parallel thinking in this area, and Oluş goes one step further: "I think gastronomy in general and wine in particular are the most important elements that reflect a society's culture and its level of socialisation, the texture of its social life."

In her home, Oluş has a specially designed dining table that sits 20 people. More than just a piece of furniture, this table has a symbolic meaning for her. She believes in the importance of gathering around a table, that food and wine connect people, they open the door to friendship, collaboration, and a better future. Oluş feels wine helps to fuel creativity like culture, she thinks it nurtures ideas and reveals the true personality of a person. How can I not agree? Like in the famous saying: "In vino veritas!" – In wine there is truth.

The table in her dining room is a great reflection of this perspective. This is also mirrored in how she created Sunolus, her beautiful boutique hotel in her vineyard. Starting with the rich local cuisine of Kayseri, Oluş paved the way to reinvigorate gastronomic culture accompanied by wine created in the cradle of the wine world. Perfectly matching a good glass of wine with the famous Kayseri dish "mantı" is now possible.

**Jumping hurdles**

Talking about values, the fact that the majority of Türkiye is dominantly Muslim has had an impact on the wine business in general. Contrary to Christianity and Judaism, where wine plays a central role with strong symbolic meanings, Islam forbids alcoholic drinks, especially wine.

Local people who are now experimenting and tasting different cuisines, such as sushi, are not necessarily open to tasting wine. Kayseri is no exception as a conservative city with strong traditional values. Religious beliefs prevent many people from consuming alcoholic drinks or getting involved in its production or business. Oluş illustrates this with an interesting example: "I met some grape growers in a regional producers' meeting a few months ago, looking to expand my supplier network. I met a grape grower there and we had a long discussion. I was aware that he wanted to become a supplier to us, selling his grapes but he was very hesitant. He had concerns around producing grapes that would be used for winemaking. I told him he did not have to drink wine, he could simply grow and sell wine grapes, which is essentially no different than growing any other fruit. He kindly nodded but walked away sadly – I knew that I was not able to convince him. Now, this is certainly a constraint, especially in my region. I believe however that this will slowly change."

It was not always like that. During the early years of the Turkish Republic, with Ataturk's support and encouragement, a state-owned alcoholic beverages production facility was created in Kayseri. With the declaration of a secular state, the first wine producers began to emerge in the Cappadocia region, reviving ancient vineyards. The demographics of the city was also not like today, as one third of the population were Christian and Armenian, making up many of the businesspeople of the city. Although wine was not commercially produced, it was made at home by many for personal consumption. Oluş says: "There was no wine trade at this time in Kayseri and no wine brands that we can mention but maybe they were exchanging wine in their own communities. Then after the independence war, in 1923, the population exchange happened and many of these people were forced to leave Türkiye. This started the period where we no longer saw wine production in Kayseri. Those who stayed used clandestine ways to produce very small amounts of wine and consume it within their family homes. This is how Kayseri lost its historical winemaking tradition."

In contrast to major Turkish cities such as Istanbul, Ankara or Izmir where wine has become a symbol of sophistication, culture and status in recent years, today Kayseri struggles to uphold its old tradition of wine production and bring consumption back. Part of the population would like to learn more and taste different wines, but the majority of the demand still comes from Turkish people who visit the region or from tourists. Based on Oluş's observations, her guests' level of education correlates with their desire to explore, understand and taste wine. These customers are keen to learn, and it is a joy to guide them on their wine journey and help them to discover and enjoy different wines.

### The unique wines of Vinolus

When I first tasted Oluş' wines a few years ago, I was impressed by their elegance. From my first sip to the end of the glass, her delicious Chardonnay reflected a very elegant style as well as her crisp Emir. Not only the wine itself, but also the bottle, the label and her brand's voice were meticulously designed. Everything was carefully crafted, almost embroidered like lace.

Indeed, Oluş's style and personality is present in every wine she produces, no doubt also fuelled by her multicultural identity. In a discussion about style, listening to Oluş, I understand that what I call her style is actually the result of a journey, where where being multicultural is at the core of everything she does: "Having a multicultural background helps me look into things with a different perspective, it also fuels my creativity because I often catch myself in an effort to combine several pieces of information when I make wine. It is just like a mosaic." It turns out in the beginning she was mainly focused on producing good quality wine. Then, she shifted to a different level where she wanted to make wines that reflect the culture of her beloved Cappadoccia. This is also the reason why she has been involved in several R&D initiatives in her 17 years of winemaking. Oluş wants to use the potential of the region to its fullest to produce authentic wines that reflect the richness and typicity of the region's terroir. "There is untapped potential in Capadoccia, the local varieties and the terroir are yet to be fully studied. I believe there is more this region can give us if we work towards it. We mainly adopt a French production style but why not combine this with the local richness and come up with new things? There is no limit in what we can do."

I believe Oluş and Turkish winemakers who share a similar mindset are building bridges with wine consumers around the world, encouraging them to discover Turkish and Cappadocian wines. Introducing them to indigenous grape varieties, to well-made local wines and to the fact that this land has an incredible history of, and a huge potential for winemaking, that in turn will make a tangible difference to the future of the Turkish wine industry. Oluş prides herself on presenting exceptional wines made from local grape varieties to her guests and customers. She loves to surprise them with her elegant wines and impress them with their quality. She says: "Many foreign visitors who come to our vineyard or stay at Vinolus do not even know that Türkiye is a wine producing country. Therefore, drinking a really good bottle of wine surprises them and I like this very much! This is the very reason why I make them try local grape varieties and our authentic blends. I am sure we have a long way to go but this is definitely worth making the effort. Once these people get to know Turkish wine, they value it very much. This is also the case with Turkish customers, they are more and more involved and curious to try different wines we make."

### Reference

Contribution of cross-cultural studies to understanding wine appreciation: A review. - H. Rodrigues and W. Parr (Food Research International, Volume 115, January 2019, Pages 251-258)

78

# The Rediscovery and Revival of Kalecik Karası: When Knowledge is Nurtured by Love

**Sabit Ağaoğlu,** *Professor of Agriculture and Owner of Tomurcukbağ Wines*

Turkish wine culture has rich and deep roots throughout history. The lands of Anatolia have hosted vineyards for thousands of years, making it one of the oldest wine-producing regions in the world. With over 1,400 indigenous grape varieties cultivated across various regions of Türkiye, the diversity and richness of the country's wine culture is unmistakable. Among these, the indigenous Kalecik Karası stands out as one of Türkiye's most important red wine grape varieties.

Benefiting from ideal climatic conditions, Kalecik Karası is renowned for its superior performance in the Kızılırmak Valley within the Kalecik district of Ankara. Wines made from this grape variety are known for their light to medium ruby-red colour with violet hues, aromatic profile and juicy, velvety mouthfeel. On the nose, floral notes flow into cherry, plum, strawberry, and forest fruits on the palate. The balance of alcohol and acidity makes it an excellent red wine to pair with meats like lamb, beef and rabbit; and cheeses such as Feta, Aged Kashkaval, Tulum Cheese, Brie or Camembert.

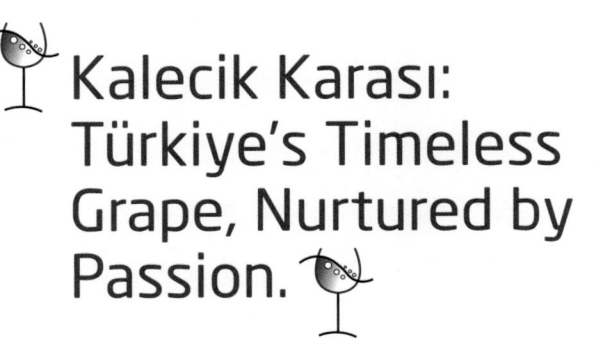

> **Kalecik Karası: Türkiye's Timeless Grape, Nurtured by Passion.**

The history of the Kalecik district dates back to 3,500-4,000 BC, having been a settlement during the Hittite, Phrygian, Galatian, Roman, Byzantine, Seljuk, Candarid, and Ottoman periods. However, despite its fertile soil, Kalecik is not utilised to its full agricultural potential today.

Kalecik Karası is one of Anatolia's most prized grape varieties. In the 1960s, vineyards across the region suffered significant damage due to phylloxera, putting this valuable grape at risk of extinction. Recognising its importance during my doctoral studies from 1965-1969, I prepared a Clone Selection project to save the Kalecik Karası grape. Since I was in Germany at the time, the project was presented to The Scientific and Technological Research Council of Türkiye (TÜBİTAK) in 1972 by the late professor, Dr. M. Nail Oraman, and other academics at the Faculty of Agriculture, Department of Viticulture and Horticulture at Ankara University, and was accepted.

Selections were made every five to six years among the vines grown in the trial vineyards of the Faculty of Agriculture, reducing the number of clones from many to twenty-three and then down to three. The second selection preserved all twenty-three clones, evaluating their winemaking characteristics. These scientific efforts, spanned approximately 19 years, ensuring the revival of the Kalecik Karası grape in Türkiye. Today, all Kalecik Karası grapes in Türkiye originate from these twenty-three clones, maintained at the Ankara University trial plots and the Kalecik Research Station.

In 1989 and 1990, we processed the grapes from these clones into wine in collaboration with the Kavaklıdere Wine Factory in Ankara. This wine was the first mono-varietal wine produced in Türkiye and was highly praised by wine enthusiasts at the time. Before this, wines produced in Türkiye were named after the regions where the grapes were grown, not the grape varieties themselves. The practice of naming wines after grape varieties began with Kalecik Karası and was later followed by other varieties like Boğazkere and Öküzgözü.

Thus, the Kalecik Karası legend began. Between 1990 and 2000, growers planted Kalecik Karası vines in various provinces, spreading the grape across the country. Unfortunately, separating the grape from its native terroir combined with several producers' commercial ambitions focusing on quantity rather than quality, led to a decline in both quality and popularity.

In the 2000s, we initiated a project with the Kalecik municipality to produce and protect Kalecik Karası. Individuals and private companies purchased land from the municipality to establish vineyards. Controlled production began, and several small and large wineries were established in Kalecik.

Oluş produces excellent wines using Kalecik Karası grapes in her Vinolus vineyards in the Cappadocia region, significantly contributing to the international recognition of this unique grape variety.

Under the leadership of Oluş, Vinolus wines are produced by skilfully combining traditional methods with modern techniques, resulting in high quality wines.

Vinolus adheres to sustainable viticulture and minimal intervention during the winemaking process, staying true to the region's heritage and uniqueness. Vinolus wines reflect the distinct terroir of Cappadocia, offering both high-quality and original wines. By promoting Kalecik Karası and Turkish wine culture on the global stage, Oluş plays a vital role in this field.

Thank you, Oluş, for your contributions to Turkish wine culture and your efforts in reviving Türkiye's indigenous grape variety, Kalecik Karası.

X14
TURCHIA | TURKEY
Yedi Bilgeler Winery
Turchia
X13
TURCHIA | TURKEY
Vinolus
X12
TURCHIA | TURKEY
Kastro Tireli
demeter

# Seeing the Unseen in Türkiye: A Precarious Heritage for Humanity

**Gözdem Gürbüzatik,** *Fermented and Distilled Beverages Strategist. Heritage Vines of Turkey Co-founder*

As a consultant in the field of fermented and distilled beverage products and innovation strategies under my brand "Fernkolektif", I closely follow the accomplishments of Türkiye's wine culture and in particular Oluş and her brand, Vinolus, which I greatly admire. As an additional endeavour, I am currently taking part in the "Anatolian Grapes Project"; a collaboration to protect ungrafted indigenous Anatolian vines in phylloxera-free vineyards.

### Cappadocia, in Central Anatolia, the home of Vinolus

Türkiye is considered the birthplace of grape domestication and winemaking. Vineyards here span from sea level to altitudes of up to 1,770 metres, highlighting both the incredible biodiversity and tradition of viticulture that has endured across several empires, from the Hittites to the Ottomans. The ongoing cultivation of vines has existed despite disruptions to Türkiye's culture and populace in the early 20th century. Nation State building, WWI, governmental changes and phylloxera have led to a general loss of cultural memory, from one generation to the next during the transition from the Ottoman Empire to the Turkish Republic. From 1923, the modern Republic focused on economic development, establishing state-wide monopolies on wine production in order to generate revenue from agriculture.

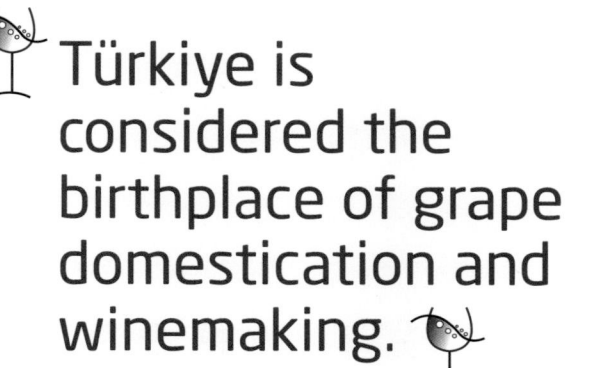

> Türkiye is considered the birthplace of grape domestication and winemaking.

During this state monopoly phase, the government initiated projects to record vine and grape varieties across Türkiye, resulting in the registration of 1,439 grape varieties, of which 854 were genetically unique, highlighting Türkiye's huge diversity. However, until only recently, the vinification of indigenous grapes was fairly limited. Privatisation in 2004 stimulated a renewed interest in winemaking, and today there are around 195 wineries in Türkiye. This renaissance is characterised by a focus on Türkiye's terroir and unique grape varieties,

III üncü MİLLETLER ARASI
## ÜZÜM, ÜZÜM SUYU ve ŞARAP
## KONGRESİ

İSTANBUL
2—5 EKKİM
1 9 4 7

with 68 indigenous varieties currently vinified. Türkiye is also the world's fifth largest in terms of land under vine, yet with the highest rate of vine loss experienced over the last 30 years, this creates a major juxtaposition with current developments.

Responding to these challenges, the non-profit initiative, The Heritage Vines of Turkey established in 2021 aims to raise awareness of individual micro-terroirs whilst protecting and promoting the country's ancient vineyards. This initiative has been crucial in both cataloguing and raising awareness for these old vineyards, ensuring that these genetic and cultural treasures find their economic and historical footing in the modern world. The project, supported by various organizations, involves mapping vineyards, conducting genomic studies, and promoting these distinctive terroirs.

Under the title "Precarious Existence of Anatolia's Old Vineyards" the project team presented the work with the support of The Old Vine Conference and the IWSC, mapping the inventory of vineyards planted with Karasakız in Çanakkale Bayramiç, inviting wine producers to the region to draw attention to this black grape variety. Additionally, the project team had the opportunity to present the micro-terroir inventory study of old vineyards in the villages of Çömelek-Karacaoğlan-Uzuncaburç in the Toros Mountains, supported by Slow Wine and the Hans Wilsdorf Foundation, to a broader audience. In another session at the Ankara University Faculty of Agriculture Department of Horticulture, the initiative of "Heritage Vines of Türkiye", in collaboration with Montpellier Grapevine Biological Resources Centre (BRC), was announced. The project team is currently preparing to launch a comprehensive study aimed at "investigating the genomic identity of Türkiye's ancient vines and local grape varieties".

The main focus of the initiative is the comparative analysis of DNA profiles of 68 local grape varieties; with the aim to map out the worldwide distribution of each of these varieties. While scientific research will determine the genomic inventory connectivity, DNA profiling of these 68 grape varieties, as currently used in wine production in Türkiye will also take place, revealing the potential to produce unique wines that reflect distinct terroir characteristics.

Another aspect of the project will provide insights into the conservation of biological diversity, resilience to climate change, and the historical development of viticulture.

Despite Just over 3% of Türkiye's vineyards currently associated with winemaking, regions like the Aegean, Central Anatolia, Thrace, and Eastern Anatolia are key areas of production, each with special characteristics, however most of the vineyards in these regions are under threat of disappearing all together.

The Turkish wine industry faces multiple challenges including limited government export support and heavy domestic regulation, which hampers the growth of a unified country-wide brand; and hinders regional solutions to establish and protect the economic value of these vineyards and wine production. In June 2013, the Government enacted sweeping legislation to amend its existing alcohol laws. In addition to this, Türkiye passed new labelling requirements for alcoholic products and increased the tax rates for alcohol and tobacco. The impact of this 2013 regulation has led winemakers to promote vineyards and grapes to consume rather than for wine production, and to focus on wine tourism developments such as wine routes and boutique hotels.

Conferences such as "Root Origin Soil" invites stakeholders to collaborate on preserving Türkiye's viticultural heritage. Despite various financial and bureaucratic obstacles, there is optimism for the future of Turkish wine, driven by collaborative efforts and a deeper understanding of the country's unique local terroirs.

**Key Points**

**Geographical and Historical Context:**
- Türkiye's diverse geography supports a rich tradition of grape cultivation.
- Historical continuity of viticulture through various empires.

**Modern Winemaking Renaissance:**

- Early 20th-century disruptions led to a loss of cultural memory.
- State monopoly period focused on economic development through wine production.
- Privatisation in 2004 reignited interest in winemaking.

**Biodiversity and Indigenous Varieties:**

- Government projects identified 1,439 grape varieties.
- Current focus on vinifying 68 indigenous grape varieties with more on upcoming scheme.

**Heritage Vines of Türkiye Initiative:**

- Efforts to map and protect old vineyards and unique terroirs.
- Collaboration with international organizations for genomic studies.

**Challenges and Opportunities:**

- Limited export support and heavy domestic regulation.
- Creative developments in promoting vineyards and grapes.
- Importance of collaboration and understanding local terroirs.

By focusing on these aspects, this article showcases the rich heritage, recent developments, and future potential of Turkish winemaking, emphasising the innovation and biodiversity across the industry.

We are still discovering our own soil and terroir. Although we make interesting, high-quality wines, in order for local varieties to establish their own unique profiles and characteristics, Türkiye's producers need to work collaboratively and support each other. There are obstacles of course, financial being the key issue, however by finding a way to work as a collective, our common goal is to grow the industry at a steady pace. All of us should work for the expansion of Türkiye's wine industry and create visibility and transparency on a global level.

Thank you for your contribution and support dear Oluş.

*Oluş, José, Kübra and Kadem in the wine cellar*

🍷 If Türkiye were to increase the percentage of grapes used for wine production from 5% to 25%, it could potentially generate around €1.845 billion in additional revenue. 🍷

# Economic Potential of the Turkish Wine Industry: From a Historical Perspective to a Future Scenario

**Yasemin Altınyay,** *International Banker*

The Ottoman Empire, which the Republic of Türkiye succeeded, is often recognised and accepted as an Islamic state. However, it was much more than that; it was a civilization built at the world's crossroads, blending numerous nations and religions within its borders.

While the Ottoman dynasty was indeed Turkish and Muslim, the characteristics of the Empire were far more complex. The transfer of the Islamic Caliphate from Egypt to Istanbul by Sultan Selim I in the 16th century is often cited as a pivotal moment that positioned the Ottoman Empire as the antithesis of Christian Europe. Yet, this view is an oversimplification.

The Ottoman administration allowed its non-Muslim subjects a degree of freedom that was, by comparison to some European states, relatively generous. Through the millet system, which was a system of governance that allowed religious and ethnic communities (millets) to govern themselves under their own laws while being loyal subjects to the Ottoman state, non-Muslim communities were granted a level of autonomy, enabling them to live their lives with minimal interference. This contrasted sharply with the rigid controls seen in contemporary European states. The Ottoman Empire, in essence, was a multicultural state situated in the very regions once heralded as the cradle of Western civilization – a reality rediscovered and romanticised by later European historians.

Non-Muslim communities in the Ottoman Empire, especially those involved in alcohol production, enjoyed relative freedom. This was a

> **Processing Turkish grapes into wine would contribute significantly to the Turkish economy and allow the revival of Turkish wines' quality to be recognized in global gastronomic culture.**

symbiotic relationship where Muslim Turks also benefited from the vibrant cultures that flourished within the Empire's borders. However, with the rise of nationalism in Europe - particularly the romantic nationalism that reawakened these dormant identities - the Ottoman Empire was targeted.

An example of this is the wine production by non-Muslims, which was not just a source of tax revenue but also a significant export commodity for the Empire. The late 19th-century phylloxera crisis, which devastated European vineyards, led to an unexpected surge in wine exports from the Ottoman Empire to countries like France, Spain, and Italy. Historical records even note attempts by French wine houses to cultivate vines in Thrace. In 1904, Ottoman wine exports to Europe reached 340 million litres—almost four times the total production of modern Türkiye.

Yet, the advent of World War I and the consequent fervour for nation-states - anchored in the triad of common language, culture, and religion - brought about a societal collapse, not just in Austria-Hungary but also, and more profoundly, in the Ottoman Empire. This collapse led to the impoverishment of many layers of its once multicultural society. The forced migration of millions of Turkish Muslims from Eastern Europe, starting with the Serbian Uprising in 1814, and the exodus of non-Muslims during and after World War I, marked the end of a multicultural era.

Gözdem Gürbüzatik, in her article within this book, underscores the losses and forgotten traditions in Turkish wine culture, largely due to the decline in awareness and appreciation for wine's commercial importance by Muslim Turks and their governments. This lack of recognition persisted until the last two decades of the 20th century, leading to the decline of Türkiye's wine culture and its significance on the global stage.

I would however like to draw the reader's attention to a different perspective on this issue and new, more recent developments. The fall of the Ottoman Empire in 1922 was not just the end of a political era on a multinational societal structure, it paved the way for the birth of the Republic of Türkiye. This new Republic embraced modernization, integrated with Western democracies, and, most importantly, granted unprecedented rights to Turkish women, achieving a relatively balanced gender equality in a Muslim society. For this, as a woman, I am grateful to Atatürk and his mother, Zübeyde Hanım.

Although the Republic of Türkiye had to forgo its multicultural heritage, it successfully integrated its society within the world and modernized it. Without this transformation, exemplary Turkish women like Oluş would not have been able to leave their mark on wine culture. The inadequacies in the Turkish wine sector today, stemming from societal and political unawareness, also need to be considered from an economic standpoint. Türkiye has the world's fifth-largest vineyard area, yet only 5% of its vineyards are dedicated to winemaking. Imagine if only 25% of the vineyards were used, what could be achieved. Of course, not every grape is suitable for winemaking, but let's do a little calculation here: if Türkiye dedicated just 25% of its grape production to winemaking rather than table grapes and exported the subsequent wine, what kind of commercial gain could be realized?

According to information from The International Organisation of Vine and Wine, the average production of wine in wine growing regions worldwide is about 56%.

Scenario: Today, Türkiye utilises only 5% of Its grape production for winemaking. Let's estimate the potential additional economic gain if Türkiye dedicated 25% of its grape production to winemaking, aligning closer to the world's average.

We can start with some assumptions based on global data. Türkiye is one of the world's largest grape producers, with approximately four million metric tonnes of grapes produced annually. As mentioned, only 5% of this production (around 200,000 tonnes) is used for winemaking. If Türkiye were to shift 25% of its grape production to winemaking, this would mean approximately one million tonnes of grapes would be used for wine production instead of just 200,000 tonnes, a fourfold increase.

On average, about 1.3 kilogrammes of grapes are needed to produce one litre of wine. Using this ratio, the additional 800,000 tonnes of grapes could potentially produce about 615 million litres of wine (800,000,000 kg / 1.3 kg per litre = 615,384,615 litres). The global average price for wine varies, however for a rough estimate, we can use an average wholesale price of €3 per litre (this figure can fluctuate of course, depending on the quality and market positioning of the wine).

Based on these assumptions, the potential revenue from 615 million additional litres of wine at €3 per litre would amount to approximately €1.845 billion (615 million litres × €3 per litre). This does not account for costs such as production, labour, and export logistics, but gives a broad sense of potential revenue.

Regarding the impact on Türkiye's Economy, we can say that the shift from table grapes to winemaking would not only provide substantial economic benefits through exports, but could also help the domestic wine industry to grow, increase tourism in grape growing regions such as Cappadocia and Thrace, and create new employment opportunities in viticultural related industries.

If Türkiye were to increase the proportion of grapes used for wine production from 5% to 25%, it could potentially generate around €1.845 billion in additional revenue from wine exports alone. This transformation would not only offer a financial boost to the economy but also elevate Türkiye's position across the global wine industry, making it a more prominent player and further integrating its agricultural economy with international markets and audiences.

To sum up, processing more Turkish grapes into wine would contribute significantly to the Turkish economy, and also revive, showcase and create recognition for the quality of Turkish wines across global gastronomic cultures. So, Oluş, and Turkish winemakers, despite all the challenges, let's create an environment for such a positive national income source.

**JRE**
JEUNES RESTAURATEURS

**50 YEARS OF NEVER-ENDING PASSION**

# The Essence of Wine in Fine Dining

JRE-Jeunes Restaurateurs, as the preeminent and most expansive international culinary association at the zenith of gastronomic excellence in Europe, perceives a boundless culinary potential within Türkiye and extends its profound expertise in this realm. With a prestigious network encompassing over 400 distinguished chefs and restaurateurs across 16 nations, and graced with more than 200 Michelin stars, JRE boasts a half-century of unparalleled experience in the evolution and refinement of culinary traditions. Our extensive knowledge and mastery particularly shine in elevating and promoting regions and domains that remain underappreciated and await discovery.

Among such treasures is Türkiye's resurgent wine heritage. Revered as the cradle of grape domestication and viniculture, Türkiye's ties to the art of winemaking stretch deep into antiquity. In recent years, concerted efforts to refine winemaking techniques and elevate quality have yielded a remarkable proliferation of Turkish wineries, now producing wines of international calibre. This work is a tribute to the extraordinary achievement of Vinolus, brought to life by Oluş Molu in the storied lands of Anatolia, particularly within the captivating region of Cappadocia, where JRE hosted a significant event, underscoring the vital role of gastrodiplomacy. The book serves as a testament to Türkiye's evolving and thriving wine industry. Esteemed gastronomic luminaries and key influencers have generously contributed their expertise to this volume, and it is through this lens that the JRE ethos is most aptly introduced.

> Wine is not simply a beverage; it is a narrative medium that enhances and complements the food on the plate.

### A Reflection on JRE-Jeunes Restaurateurs and Their Gastronomic Philosophy

In the realm of fine dining, the interplay between cuisine and wine transcends mere consumption; it is a sophisticated dialogue between

**Hans van Manen**, Secretary General of the JRE

culture, history, and the senses. JRE-Jeunes Restaurateurs, an association of visionary young Chefs and restaurateurs, exemplifies this philosophy, where the culinary arts and oenology converge to create a holistic dining experience. The essence of JRE's approach to fine dining lies in its commitment to innovation, sustainability, and a profound respect for tradition, with wine serving as a pivotal element in their gastronomic narrative.

### JRE-Jeunes Restaurateurs: A Commitment to Excellence

Founded in 1974, JRE-Jeunes Restaurateurs brings together some of the most talented young Chefs and restaurateurs across Europe, united by a shared passion for excellence in gastronomy. The organisation's members are not only adept at crafting exquisite dishes but are also innovators, pushing the boundaries of culinary arts. The JRE philosophy emphasises creativity, local produce, and a deep connection to the terroir—the natural environment in which food and wine are cultivated. This connection is crucial, as it grounds their culinary creations in a sense of place and history, making each dining experience unique and authentic.

### The Integral Role of Wine in Fine Dining

In top gastronomy, wine is not simply a beverage; it is a narrative medium that enhances and complements the food on the plate. Wine, like cuisine, is a product of its environment, reflecting the climate, soil, and traditions of its region. This concept of terroir is central to both winemaking and haute cuisine, making wine an indispensable part of any dining experience. The selection of wine in fine dining is a meticulous process, involving the

Sommelier who understands the intricate relationships between various wines and the dishes they accompany. The right pairing can elevate a meal, bringing out hidden flavours and creating a harmonious balance that lingers on the palate. In this sense, wine becomes an extension of the Chef's artistry, a liquid expression of the same principles that guide the creation of the food.

### The Symbiosis of Wine and Food: A Sensory Dialogue

The relationship between wine and food in fine dining is one of symbiosis, where each element enhances the other. This symbiotic relationship is carefully curated by the Sommelier, who understand that a dish and its accompanying wine must be in perfect harmony to achieve the desired gastronomic effect. A well-paired wine can accentuate the subtle nuances of a dish, bringing out flavours that might otherwise go unnoticed, while the food can soften the tannins or highlight the fruitiness of the wine.

Moreover, wine in fine dining is not just about flavour; it is also about creating a sensory experience that engages all the senses. The colour, aroma, and texture of wine add layers of complexity to a meal, inviting diners to explore the depth of each component. This sensory engagement is at the heart of the philosophy, where dining is not just about eating but about experiencing the full spectrum of joy and, what food and wine can offer.

### Tradition and Innovation: The Dual Pillars of JRE's Philosophy

While Chefs are innovators, they are also deeply rooted in tradition. This duality is reflected in their approach to wine, where traditional winemaking techniques are often paired with contemporary culinary practices. The result is a dining experience that honours the past while looking towards the future, creating a bridge between generations and cultures. Wine, with its rich history and cultural significance, plays a crucial role in this dialogue between tradition and innovation. Many Chefs and Sommeliers collaborate closely with local winemakers, selecting wines that not only complement their dishes but also tell the story of the region's heritage. This collaboration ensures that each meal is a reflection of both the Chef's creativity and the winemaker's craft, making wine an integral part of the narrative that top restaurants seek to convey.

> **Dining is not just about eating but about experiencing the full spectrum of joy that food and wine can offer.**

### The Art of Fine Dining

In the world of JRE-Jeunes Restaurateurs, wine and food are more than just sustenance; they are expressions of art, culture, and philosophy. The association's commitment to excellence, innovation, and tradition is mirrored in their approach to wine, which plays a central role in creating a memorable dining experience. For JRE, fine dining is not just about what is on the plate or in the glass, but about the stories they tell, the emotions they evoke, and the sensory journey they offer to those who partake. In this way, JRE-Jeunes Restaurateurs elevates dining to an art form, where wine and cuisine are inextricably linked, creating a harmonious symphony that resonates with the very essence of gastronomy.

*Oluş with her core team: (from left to right) Muhsin Tınık, Metin Unutkan, Furkan Dönmez, Kübranur Birtek, Kadem Güvenç, Oluş, Eka Torchinava, Bülent Bilgiç, Ali Akşahin.*